Social Problems of the Industrial Revolution

Other titles in preparation:

Economic Problems of the Industrial Revolution
Documents of the Industrial Revolution
The Revolution in Agriculture

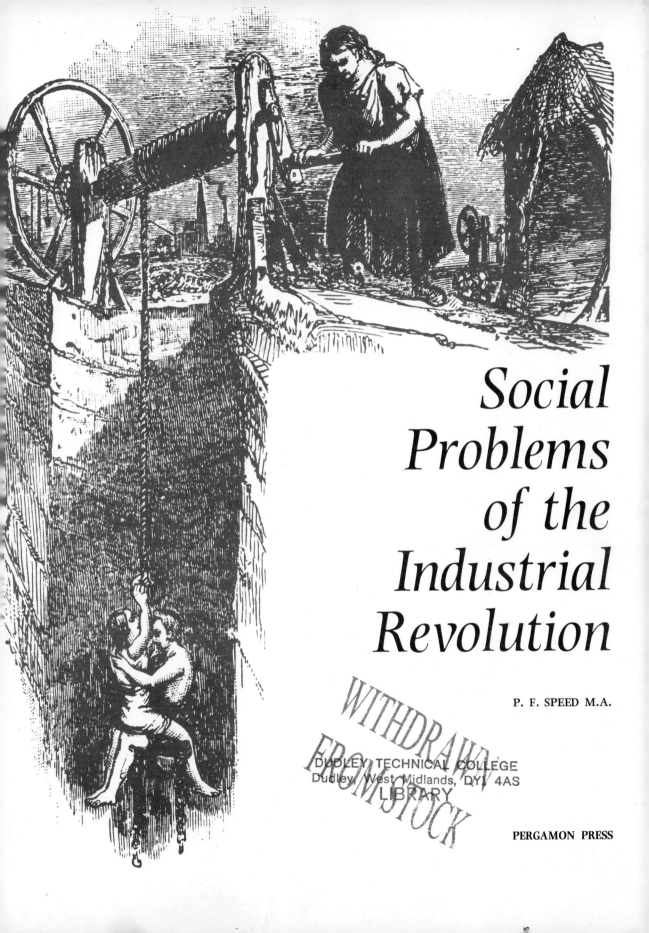

Social
Problems
of the
Industrial
Revolution

P. F. SPEED M.A.

PERGAMON PRESS

Pergamon Press Ltd, Headington Hill Hall,
Oxford OX3 OBW
Pergamon Press Inc., Maxwell House, Fairview
Park, Elmsford, New York 10523
Pergamon of Canada Ltd, PO Box 9600, Don Mills,
Ontario, M3C 2T9
Pergamon Press (Aust.) Pty Ltd, 19a Boundary
Street, Rushcutters Bay, N.S.W. 2011, Australia

First edition 1975

Printed in Great Britain by A. Wheaton & Co.,
Exeter

ISBN 0 08 017810 3 net
ISBN 0 08 018883 4 non-net

Contents

Introduction

BRITAIN WAS THE FIRST COUNTRY IN THE WORLD TO DEVELOP HER INDUSTRY ON A LARGE scale. The changes came quickly upon a society that was bewildered and ill-equipped to deal with them. Not surprisingly, industrialisation brought with it social problems such as slum housing, crime, poverty and ignorance on a scale not met before, together with a deterioration in public health. This book describes these and other problems but also shows how, at the same time, there were people who responded to the challenge and dedicated themselves to social reform.

Population changes and the Industrial Revolution

WE USUALLY UNDERSTAND THE TERM 'INDUSTRIAL REVOLUTION' TO MEAN THE CHANGES that took place in the life and work of the people of Great Britain during the late eighteenth and early nineteenth centuries.

One of the most remarkable things about this period was a rapid growth in the population. Unfortunately we have no reliable figures before the first census of 1801, but there was a careful estimate made by Gregory King in 1695. He gave the population then as 5.5 million for England and Wales. By 1801 it was 9.3 million, and by 1841 15.9 million.

There are two things that decide whether a population is going to increase: its birth rate and its death rate. If many babies are born the population is likely to rise, but not if, at the same time, people are dying in equally large numbers. The important thing is the difference between the birth rate and the death rate. The wider the gap, the more rapid is the growth of population.

There has been a lot of research on the birth and death rates during the eighteenth century, but because no one recorded births and deaths accurately, it is impossible to be sure of what happened. However most historians agree on the following points.

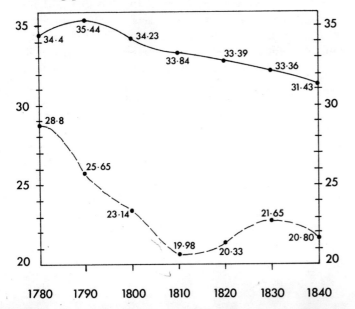

Birth and death rates per thousand 1780–1840

Birth Rate

- - - - - -

Death Rate

Birth and death rates

In the first place there was a high birth rate, and this may even have increased as time went on, though not to a great extent. Secondly, there was a fall in the death rate. Quite when it began is not clear, but it seems to have been considerable. Along with the high birth rate, it was enough to cause a 'population explosion'. How can we explain this fall in the death rate?

In previous centuries people had died because of famine. In the eighteenth century there were occasionally bad harvests and food was sometimes short, but there was no famine. This was the time of the agricultural revolution, when farmers were bringing more land into cultivation and using improved methods. Not only did they produce more food, but it was of better quality. One of the most hopeful changes was the cultivation of turnips and grass crops which made it possible to keep stock alive through the winter. In the old days, many animals had been slaughtered in the autumn, and the meat salted down. Now it was possible to have fresh meat and a good supply of milk all the year round. Milk is especially important for babies and young children, who had formerly died in large numbers.

Along with famines, epidemics had been great killers, particularly the plague or Black Death. There was no more plague after 1679 though why is not at all clear. Another, though less important, disease that vanished mysteriously was malaria, or the ague as it was sometimes called. Many diseases remained, particularly dangerous ones being typhus and smallpox, but it seems that even these began to decline.

Possibly the increased use of cotton helped to get rid of typhus. Because wool is not easy to wash, and cannot be boiled, it stayed dirty and lice thrived in it. In the later part of the eighteenth century cheap cotton goods became common, and cotton is easy to wash, while boiling it is the best way to clean it. Washing, particularly boiling, killed lice and checked the spread of typhus.

Perhaps the decline of smallpox was a result of the discovery of inoculation. Lady Mary Wortley Montagu brought the idea from the Middle East in 1722. The usual way to carry out inoculation was to find someone suffering from smallpox and draw a thread through one of his sores. The doctor would then make a slight cut on the arm of the person to be inoculated and draw the thread through that in turn. If all went well the patient would have a mild attack of smallpox and thereafter be immune, but there were dangers. Possibly the attack of smallpox would be severe and the patient would die. Yet even if the attack was slight, it was genuine smallpox and it could be passed to others. It is difficult to say how effective inoculation was in cutting down deaths from smallpox and probably the really hopeful change only came after 1798 when Jenner discovered vaccination. By this method the patient is given an injection of cowpox germs which are most unlikely to hurt him, but will make him immune to smallpox for at least some years.

To sum up so far, we have seen that during the late eighteenth century and early nineteenth century there was a rapid increase in the population, which seems to have been due mainly to a fall in the death rate. This came about because there was a decline in famine and plague and other epidemic diseases.

But then there was a check to progress. In about 1815 the death rate stopped falling and, in fact, it increased slightly. It did not start to fall again until after 1870. Obviously something had gone wrong, and we can get some idea as to what it was if we look not only at the increase of the population, but also at changes in its distribution.

Between 1801 and 1841 the population of the whole country rose by about 60 per cent, but the large towns grew by nearly 140 per cent. Individual towns grew even faster than this, as we can see from Manchester and Bradford. In the sixty years before 1831, Manchester increased its size six times. Bradford grew by 50 per cent every ten years between 1811 and 1851, and by that time only half the people living in the town had been born there.

Before the Industrial Revolution, most of the people of England and Wales lived in the countryside; by 1851, half of them were town dwellers. From being a farming country we had become the first nation in the world to be mainly industrial. This was one of the most important developments in our history, but it brought its problems.

ORIGINAL SOURCES

Malthus. *Essay on Population.*

FURTHER READING

Buer, M. C. *Health, Wealth and Population in the Early Days of the Industrial Revolution.* Routledge, London, 1968.
Flinn, M. W. *British Population Growth 1700–1850.* Studies in Economic History, Macmillan, London, 1970. This is a pamphlet with an excellent bibliography, and the best short introduction to the subject.
Hare, Ronald. *Pomp and Pestilence.* Gollancz, London, 1954.

LITERARY SOURCES
Dickens, Charles, Great Expectations. Penguin, Harmondsworth, 1969. (Chapters 1 and 2: infant mortality.)

2 The state of the towns

Town planning

We saw in the last chapter how quickly the population of the towns grew. This meant that builders had to put up houses quickly. Moreover, these houses had to be cheap since many people could not afford to pay more than two shillings a week in rent. This is the budget a landlord might expect if he had a house in Ashton-under-Lyne, Lancashire:

Expenses:		
Annual ground rent	6s	3d
Poor rates	4s	6d
Water rent	6s	0d
Repairs (average for first twenty years)	11s	3d
Annual loss $22\frac{1}{2}$% (caused by bad tenants and houses standing empty)	£1 3s	4d
Total expenses	£2 11s	4d
Annual rent, at two shillings a week	£5 4s	0d
Annual expenses	£2 11s	4d
Annual profit	£2 12s	8d

The landlord would want a profit of between 5 and 6 per cent on the capital invested in the house. If the profit is only £2 12s 8d, then the house must not cost more than £50. Even in those days £50 was not much for a house. Cheap houses are usually bad, and what made things even worse in those days was that no one oversaw the builders. In the early nineteenth century local authorities had little power to interfere, and indeed, many of them did not want to anyway.

Since they were free to do more or less as they pleased, builders crammed as many houses as they could into the smallest possible spaces. They found that they could save land by building their houses not only in terraces but back to back as well. Back to back houses first appeared in the late eighteenth century, and by the 1840s they were common in many towns. For example, in Nottingham at this time there were about 11 000 houses and over 7000 of them were back to back.

There were many miles of streets with these dismal little houses, but even worse than the streets were the courts. This is a plan of a typical court:

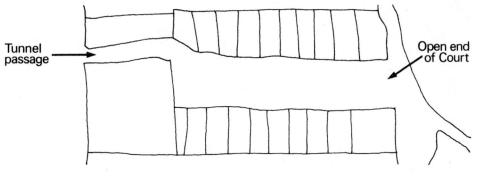

Tunnel passage → / Open end of Court

A Court

The open end might be wide enough for a cart to pass through, but not always. Some courts were so narrow that a man could touch the houses on both sides with his arms stretched out. In them the sun rarely shone, and the air was stale.

Parks and gardens were rare. Someone said of Manchester:

> *There are no public walks or places of recreation by which the thousands of labourers or their families can relieve the tedium of their monotonous employment. Pent up in a close, dusty atmosphere from half past five or six o'clock in the morning, till seven or eight o'clock at night, from week to week, without change, without inter- mission, it is not to be wondered at that they fly to the spirit and beer shops and the dancing houses.*
>
> *Manchester is singularly destitute of these resources which conduce at once to health and recreation. With a teeming population she has no public walks or resorts for the community to snatch an hour's enjoyment.* (Edwin Chadwick, *Report on the Sanitary Condition of the Labouring Population of Great Britain*, p. 336.)

By 1846 Manchester was, in fact, lucky enough to have a park, but at that time no other large town except London had one.

Construction of working class houses

The builders not only saved land, they also saved materials. By now many building materials were cheap. Brickmakers had plenty of coal, cheap slates came from Wales, and cheap softwood from Scandinavia. Thanks to the railways and the canals, merchants could send bulky goods quite easily to any large town in the British Isles.

Builders can, of course, make excellent houses with these materials if they use them properly, but in those days they did not take proper care when they were putting up houses for the poor. Outside walls had no cavities to keep out the wet and the cold, and even worse, there were no damp-courses, so that moisture crept up the walls making them damp and black to a height of about three feet. Down- stairs, the floors were often made of bricks, resting on the earth, and were damp,

Working class houses

A court in Glasgow. This photograph shows a typical court of the first half of the nineteenth century. The camera is pointing towards the tunnel entrance. Note the kennel in the middle of the street, which was the only drain or sewer they had, and the solitary stand pipe that would have supplied all the houses with their water. Courtesy of Mansell Collection.

cold and difficult to clean. Foundations were weak, so that the walls often cracked; roofs often leaked since the builders used as little timber as they dared and made the slates overlap the smallest amount possible. The joinery was poor; doors and windows did not fit, so that they either stuck, or else were loose.

The plans were simple. In the £50 house there was one room downstairs, and one upstairs – that was all. Larger houses would have a second bedroom over the first, and there might also be a cellar. There was no entrance hall, so that the street door opened into the living room, and there was no kitchen. Not only were bathrooms unheard of, but no house had a lavatory of its own. The only storage space was under the stairs, where the tenant might have to keep his food along with his coal.

Quite often there was a pigsty outside the door, so that the smell of pig manure mingled with the smell of human manure in the privies, cesspools and dung heaps.

Sanitation

Sanitation was bad for the water closet was still a luxury. Some of the poor had to make do with a wooden bar wedged across the corner of a yard, but usually they had a privy which would just be a shed with a wooden seat inside, below which was a cesspit. When the cesspit was full, workmen emptied it by hand and took the sloppy mess away in carts that dripped and leaked as they made their way through the town. The smell this made was so unpleasant that it was unlawful to do it by day – hence those who did the work were called 'night men'. Only the most degraded would take such a job and they were not too careful how they went about it. If they found a cesspit that was difficult to empty, they broke down its wall or smashed the seat of the privy.

London nightmen. These were the men whose job was to empty cesspits. The stench they raised was so unpleasant that they were only allowed to work at night.
Courtesy of Guildhall Library, City of London.

7

Sanitation

Living near a cesspit was unpleasant. Sometimes a house stood partly over a privy; sometimes a cesspit was against the wall of a house, and the contents would soak through. In one house, Lord Shaftesbury visited a family living in a basement where the smell was overpowering. He lifted one of the floor boards to find out why and discovered a huge cesspit just underneath.

Few privies were clean. There would perhaps be a block of six to a court of some forty houses, each house having nine inhabitants on average. No one wanted the job of cleaning the privies and so they stayed filthy. But the real trouble was when the cesspits were full for it cost £1 to empty one — ten weeks rent for a house. This was a lot of money, and landlords were none too keen to pay it. The result was that the cesspits overflowed, and the sewage ran down the streets. We hear of courts so full of liquid filth that the inhabitants put down stepping stones to make their way through it; we hear of houses with sewage oozing up through the floors; we hear of the subsoil being soaked so thoroughly that the houses were standing on land as foul as a manure heap.

Sometimes the inhabitants of a court would make a little money by piling their dung into heaps and then selling it to 'muck majors'. These folk stacked the manure in monstrous heaps, and left it to rot. There was one other way to get rid of refuse, and that was simply to dump it in front of the house and leave it. The town council would send scavengers into some streets to take it away, but elsewhere it would have to evaporate, rot or wash away with the rain.

As far back as the reign of Henry VIII there was an Act of Parliament which set up Commissioners of Sewers for various districts and it was their responsibility to raise money out of the local rates and build sewers. But it was not part of the original plan to use the sewers to carry away refuse. They were there to stop flooding by taking away storm water and it was only later that people began to build house drains and connect these to the sewers.

Watering the Streets. Woodcut from Dr Shapter's book 'The History of the Cholera in Exeter'.

Even if a street was lucky enough to have a sewer, it did not follow that its sanitation troubles were over. Quite often there were no drains connecting the houses to the sewers, as these were expensive, and householders and landlords did not want to pay for them. It might even be against the law to build a house drain, as at Liverpool, where people were not supposed to connect a water closet drain to a sewer. It was quite right to stop them linking up with cesspools, since all sorts of rubbish went into them which could easily block a sewer, but to extend the rule to water closets was unreasonable.

Only too often the sewers did not work. Builders made them without first having a proper survey, so that they were level, or nearly so, and could not drain. They were also expensive: workmen built them laboriously with bricks, since there were no pipes such as we use now. As a result they cost eleven shillings a foot and many towns could not afford all the sewers they needed. By a great effort Manchester had built thirty-two miles of sewers by 1830, but this still left nearly half the town without. Things were much worse in Liverpool where there were only eleven miles of sewers, and these were in the wealthiest areas that needed them least.

The streets

From what we have seen of the sanitation it is obvious that the streets were not pleasant. Some indeed had drains and good paved surfaces so that it was not too difficult to keep them clean. Others had no underground drains, but were well paved. It was possible to sweep a street like this and, if it was on a slope, a good storm of rain would take away a lot of the filth. These streets usually had a kennel down the middle. ('Kennel' is the word 'canal' or 'channel' in another form.) It was a wide, deep gutter into which people put their refuse and poured their slops, while rain-water also ran along it.

But if a street was low-lying, unpaved and undrained, then it was indeed foul. Much of the time it would be deep in mud and slush with evil-smelling, stagnant pools, the colour of stale beer. A Manchester doctor wrote:

> *Whole streets, unpaved and without drains or main sewers, are worn into deep ruts and holes in which water constantly stagnates, and are so covered with refuse and excrementitious matter as to be almost impassable from depth of mud and intolerable from stench.* (Chadwick, op. cit., p. 111.)

Water supplies

The poor suffered because of bad drainage. They also suffered because of bad water supplies. The wretched inhabitants of Bermondsey Island in London lived over a swamp and they filled their buckets by letting them down from their houses. But since they flung all their refuse into the swamp, they were drinking their own sewage.

Other people collected rain-water and kept it in tubs outside their houses. The rain had fallen through air that was heavy with smoke, and the water collected slime and more dirt in the tubs. It was absolutely black. Sometimes there was a well

9

with a pump over it in the street and this could be foul from water seeping into it from cesspits and graveyards.

But most of the town water came from works owned by water companies, many of which did not do their job properly. In London some of them took their water straight out of the Thames and pumped it, untreated, along the mains and into the houses. Since the London sewers emptied themselves into the Thames, the companies were supplying diluted sewage as drinking water. Also, Thames water is very hard – twenty-six tons of lime came through the taps of London every day.

The London water companies did not supply their water constantly. The best any of them did was to run it for a while each day and others only turned it on three times a week, and then for only two hours at a time. This was bad enough for rich people who could afford to have large cisterns in their houses which filled up – if they were lucky – when the water came on. Poor people could not afford these cisterns so they collected their water in any cans and buckets that they had and kept it in their houses. Nor could they collect their water in peace, and take as much as they wanted, as there was usually only one stand-pipe to each court. When the water came on, a shout would go up and everyone would rush to get what he could, knowing that there might only be half an hour. One man counted over sixty people round a tap. There was often quarrelling and fighting, so that the police often had to come in.

Under these conditions most people did not even try to keep clean. They were dirty, their clothes were dirty, their houses were dirty, and they smelled abominably.

Not all the water companies were as bad as those in London. Nottingham was a lucky town for here the Trent Water Company supplied about 36 000 people. It took pure water from sand and gravel beds, filtered it and pumped it into a water tower high up in the town. From here it flowed along the water mains under pressure.

In Greenock, Paisley and Ayr they also had constant supplies of good clean water due to filtering. But all in all, it was still a luxury to have in a house a constant supply of clear, fresh water.

Cellar dwellings

We have already seen that some houses had cellars and usually the family who rented the house sub-let their cellar. If it was dry and had a window and fireplace, then a cellar dwelling might not be too bad. But most cellars were damp, and often both the land around them, and the street above them were foul with the overflow from the cesspits. Filthy liquid oozed up through the floor or dripped down the steps. All the inhabitants could do was to dig a hole so that at least it collected in one place. Sometimes they had to take the door off its hinges and prop it on bricks, so that they could have somewhere dry to rest.

One of the worst towns for cellar dwellings was Liverpool. In 1839 there were 7860 inhabited cellars there, with 39 000 people living in them. This was one-seventh of the whole population of the town. Well over half of these cellars were not fit to live in as they did not have any windows, fireplaces or their own outside doors.

Lodging houses · Local government

Lodging houses

Some families could not even afford to live in cellars, and they crowded into the poor lodging houses. Here there was every sort of misery, disease, and wickedness: there were thieves, tramps, beggars, prostitutes, drunkards, idlers of all kinds, and mixed with them, honest families who had fallen on hard times.

Men, women and children slept, ate, dressed and undressed in the same room. The landlords crammed the beds in as tightly as they could, and then allowed as many lodgers as possible into each bed. Sometimes there were no beds, but only straw or shavings on the floor.

The rooms were rarely cleaned, the bedclothes were hardly ever washed. Usually there were people sleeping during the day as well as at night, and no one would open a window. The smell of the heated, unwashed bodies made the air so foul that anyone not used to such rooms could not go through the door.

Burial grounds

There were two sorts of burial ground, both equally bad. Some belonged to the parish churches and others to private companies, who made money out of them. The main problem was that these graveyards were too crowded, and too close to crowded houses so that they poisoned the air, the ground, and the wells used for drinking water.

Local government

The towns were in disorder, because local government was in disorder, but we would be wrong to think that there were no local authorities. They were inefficient, but there were plenty of them. One problem was, as we shall see, that there were too many.

First of all there were the Justices of the Peace. There had been Justices since the Middle Ages, but they had become especially important under the Tudors. They were still important in the early nineteenth century. When they met in the Quarter Sessions they could make regulations, but they were unpaid amateurs, and they had so many duties that they could not possibly do them all properly. They did not have the technical knowledge to cope with sanitation and water supplies and, above all, they did not have the power to make a good job of cleaning the towns. Industrial towns as big as Manchester and Birmingham were still being administered by Justices as late as 1839.

Towns which had charters were called Municipal Boroughs and had mayors with usually 'closed' corporations. Today the members of a town council are elected. Before 1835 the existing council members chose new members, and of course they picked men who were of the same mind as themselves. Councillors paid little attention to the opinions of the other citizens and many of them cared little for the general good of the town that they were supposed to govern.

In the eighteenth and nineteenth centuries, water companies began to appear. A group of people would put their money together and then petition Parliament for an Act giving them the right to supply water to a town, and, of course, charge their

11

customers for it. The Trent Water Company's Act was in 1752. We have already seen that some water companies served their towns well, but there were many who thought more about a good profit for their shareholders than about good water for their customers.

The more progressive towns asked Parliament to pass local Improvement Acts. These Acts varied and each one suited the needs, or perhaps just the fancies, of the town that had asked for it. Usually an Improvement Act would set up one or more *ad hoc* boards. An *ad hoc* board deals with one particular problem, such as drainage, or scavenging, or paving. Obviously no *ad hoc* board would be responsible for the general welfare of a town in the way that a modern town council is.

We can see how confused local government was by looking at London in the 1840s. Here there were no less than seven Commissioners of Sewers and nine water companies. In the parish of St Pancras alone there were sixteen Paving Boards acting under twenty-nine Acts of Parliament. Altogether in the Metropolitan area, outside the City, there were over three hundred local authorities of one kind or another.

There could be no regulated and orderly government and sanitation in a town while its authorities were as confused as this.

The Public Health Movement

As we have already seen earlier in this chapter, individual towns had been making spasmodic attempts to improve themselves from the eighteenth century onwards. But there was no organised public health movement until the early nineteenth century, when a civil servant called Edwin Chadwick began to take an interest in the problem. Chadwick was Secretary to the Poor Law Board which had been set up in 1834 and his work here showed him that disease was one of the main causes of poverty. From time to time disquieting reports came in from the Medical Officers of the new Poor Law Unions, and there had also been some investigations by three men – Doctors Kay, Southwood Smith and Arnott. Chadwick urged the need for a more systematic enquiry until 1839 when Parliament authorised him to collect information from all over the country, and to prepare a report. Chadwick worked hard at this for two years, so that in 1842 he published his findings in his *Report on the Sanitary Conditions of the Labouring Population*. In it he set out the evils described earlier in this chapter, showing quite clearly the connection between filthy living conditions and disease. He urged strong Government action to bring sanitation reform, and refuted the idea that it would be too expensive. Disease, he said, cost far more than sanitation ever would, and even the working classes could pay their share. Piped water and sewers would add a few pence a week to the rent of a house – but working class people could hardly object to this when they were spending about £2 a year, per head, on drink and tobacco.

Chadwick had little faith in doctors. He saw no point in trying to cure diseases; it was much better to prevent them, and this, he said, could be done by efficient sewers, pure water supplies, and good houses. With his logical mind he saw one problem, and one solution. In the countryside the fields were often waterlogged and farmers were short of manure; in the towns, water was desperately short and dung

Sir Edwin Chadwick, 1800–1880. Chadwick was a key figure in social reform, especially poor law and public health. For an account of his life and work see chapters Two and Six and page 178. The portrait gives some idea of those aspects of his character which made him unpopular and so made his work much less effective than it would otherwise have been.
Courtesy of Radio Times Hulton Picture Library.

lay piled in the streets. The towns needed water from the countryside; the country-side needed manure from the towns. The land should be drained, the water purified and then brought into the towns. After use, it would scour out the sewers, and the liquid manure could be piped out to the fields.

The *Sanitary Report* was an instant success and over 30 000 copies were sold or given away. It did, however, have one weakness in that it was published under Chadwick's name, so that it did not have the authority of an official document.

The Public Health Movement

What the report did do, however, was to force the reluctant Home Secretary, Sir James Graham, to appoint a Royal Commission, known as the Health of Towns Commission, to look into the state of the towns. The Commissioners heard the evidence of all sorts of people – surveyors, engineers, architects, Poor Law officials, the Professor of Chemistry of Aberdeen University, the Chief of the London Fire Brigade and a Leicestershire stocking-weaver, who was dying of tuberculosis in absolute poverty. Chadwick was not himself a member of the Commission, but he was the man who really directed the enquiry. He selected the witnesses, chose the questions, and guided the Commissioners when they went on their tours of inspection. Not surprisingly, when the Commission reported in 1844, it endorsed everything Chadwick had said in his report of 1842.

There was a good deal of agitation amongst members of the public to press Parliament to take some action. Chadwick, as a civil servant, could not take an active part in this, but there were many enthusiasts who could and did. In December 1844 a group of them formed the Health of Towns Association, two notable members being the great philanthropist Lord Ashley (who succeeded to the peerage as Lord Shaftesbury in 1851) and Dr Southwood Smith. The Association worked hard and did not let the general public forget the importance of sanitary reform. Indeed the Health of Towns Commission showed such a bad state of affairs that the Government should at once have taken steps to put them right, but it was not until 1848 that anything was done. In that year Lord Morpeth introduced an important Bill into Parliament which, when it became law, was known as the Public Health Act.

The Act created a central authority, the General Board of Health, which consisted of three commissioners. The duty of this Board was to supervise the work of the Local Boards of Health that were to be set up under the Act. Forty clauses set out the duties of the Local Boards. They had to appoint a clerk, a treasurer, an inspector of nuisances, a surveyor and, if they wished, a medical officer of health. They had to ensure that no houses were built without drains or lavatories, and where an existing house was near a sewer, it had to be connected. The Local Board could supply water, if there was no water company, and where a company existed, then the Board could see that it did its work properly. If water could be supplied for twopence a week, then the Board could compel a householder to have it piped into his house. To pay for all these improvements, the Local Board had the right to levy a rate.

The Act was a great step forward, even though it did not give as much power to the General Board as Chadwick wanted, and even though it did not apply to London. The composition of the Board, on the other hand, pleased him. Lord Morpeth was its president, Lord Ashley was one of the Commissioners and Chadwick himself was the third. Dr Southwood Smith was the Board's Chief Medical Inspector. Chadwick felt that the way was clear for a vigorous attack on the problems of public health.

The Board could act if the death rate in any area was over 23 per 1000, or if one-tenth of the ratepayers sent in a petition. However, it very rarely used its compulsory powers under the first of these clauses, but preferred to work with local people, and win them over by friendly persuasion. Quite a number of towns took advantage of the new Public Health Act. They found that they could have good water supplies and sewers quite cheaply. Barnard Castle had constant water and proper sewers at a cost of $2\frac{1}{2}d$ a week to each ratepayer. At Ottery St Mary they had this for less than one penny a week. There was, of course, the extra cost of improving the houses, each one needing at least a sink and a W.C. but even with this the average cost worked out at no more than $3\frac{1}{2}d$ a week for each house.

The sewers favoured by the Board of Health were tubular, and made of glazed earthenware. They cost only 1s 9d a foot to lay, as against 11s a foot for the older type of brick sewer. They were more efficient too, for as long as there was a good supply of water to flush them, they were self-cleansing. This system spread rapidly; in 1848 there were only just 100 miles of pipe sewers in use, but by 1854 there were 2600 miles. The results of all this were quite spectacular in some areas, for there were places where the death rate fell to less than one half of what it had been.

But in spite of this success, all was not well. The tubular sewers were not always satisfactory. Manufacturers made them of different sizes, and with a variety of joints. Workmen joined up pipes that did not match, causing leaks or obstructions. Sometimes the sewers did not fall steeply enough so that they choked; sometimes they cracked, because they had been laid in sandy soil without enough protection from traffic passing overhead. The worst disaster came in Croydon where there was a new system which was a model of what Chadwick wanted. In 1852 there was a serious outbreak of typhoid fever – all along the line of the new sewers and water pipes. What had happened was that the contractor had made a bad job of laying both, and sewage had seeped into the water. It was Chadwick who had to take much of the blame.

Chadwick's career ended in 1854. His intentions were good, but unfortunately he had a gift for making enemies. These people could not remove him directly, but they could destroy the General Board of Health. In 1854 the Board's term of office was due for renewal, and Chadwick's opponents in Parliament decided that this should not happen. There were enough of them to swing the vote against the General Board and Chadwick was driven into retirement at the age of fifty-four. The Public Health Movement did not end with Chadwick. Without his drive it did not move as fast as it might have done, but there was progress, for example, the building of London's main drainage works, which the Prince of Wales opened in 1865. In 1885 there was another Commission on the housing of the working classes, very like the one of 1844. Lord Shaftesbury, now eighty-four years old, came to give evidence. He admitted that many of the old evils remained, particularly overcrowding, but he went on to talk about the improved sanitation, the new water supplies, and the rebuilding, like the opening of the Embankment. 'The health of London,' he said, 'has vastly improved.'

ORIGINAL SOURCES

Chadwick, Edwin. *Report on the Sanitary Condition of the Labouring Population of Great Britain.* 1842. (Now edited by M. W. Flinn in an edition published by the Edinburgh University Press, Edinburgh, 1965.)
Report of the Commissioners Inquiring into the State of the Large Towns and Populous Districts. Parliamentary Papers, 1844.

15

The State of Towns

The aim of these two reports was to expose evil conditions.

Engels, F. *The Condition of the Working Class in England*. (Trans. and edited by W. H. Chaloner and W. O. Henderson, Blackwell, Oxford, 1958.)

FURTHER READING

Dyos, H. J. and Wolff, Michael, eds. *The Victorian City: Images and Realities*. 2 vols. Routledge, London, 1973.

Finer, S. E. *The Life and Times of Edwin Chadwick*. Methuen, London, 1970.

Lewis, R. A. *Edwin Chadwick and the Public Health Movement*. Longman, London, 1952.

LITERARY SOURCES

Dickens, Charles. *Bleak House*. Penguin, Harmondsworth, 1971. (Chapter 11: a pauper's burial; chapter 16: a cemetery; chapters 16, 22 and 46: slums.)

Dickens, Charles. *Dombey and Son*. Penguin, Harmondsworth, 1970. (Chapter 6: working class houses.)

Dickens, Charles. *Nicholas Nickleby*. Blackie, Glasgow, 1962. (Chapter 14: a tenement.)

Dickens, Charles. *Oliver Twist*. Penguin, Harmondsworth, 1970. (Chapter 50; Jacob's Island – slums.)

Dickens, Charles. *The Uncommercial Traveller*. Everyman's Library, Dent, London, 1969. (Chapter 32: poverty in East London.)

Gaskell, Elizabeth. *Mary Barton*. Penguin, Harmondsworth, 1970. (Chapter 2: mill workers' houses; chapter 6: a pauper's burial, slums and cellar dwellings.)

Gaskell, Elizabeth. *North and South*. Penguin, Harmondsworth, 1970. (Chapter 7: general impressions of Manchester.)

Kingsley, Charles. *Alton Locke*. Everyman's Library, Dent, London, 1970. (Chapter 35: sewage and water supplies.)

Disease   3

IN CHAPTER ONE WE SAW HOW RAPIDLY THE POPULATION OF THIS COUNTRY INCREASED
and that this increase was probably due mainly to a fall in the death rate. Yet after
1815 the death rate stopped falling and it did not go down again until 1870. Something had gone wrong, and it was connected with the rapid growth of the towns.
We can see what this meant from the table below.

Average ages of death in Liverpool and Rutlandshire, 1840

Class	Liverpool	Rutlandshire
Professional or gentry	35	52
Tradesmen	22	41
Labourers and artisans	15	38

Two things are clear: the rich lived longer than the poor, and country people
lived longer than townsfolk. A farm worker in Rutland would hope to live slightly
longer than a solicitor in Liverpool, and more than twice as long as a Liverpool
factory worker. The town poor died young, and, after what we have seen of the
cities, this is hardly surprising. What were the diseases that were killing them?

The most spectacular, and the most dreaded disease of our period, was cholera.
Cholera's home is India, especially the filthy, miserable delta of the river Ganges,
and several times during the nineteenth century an epidemic left India to spread
like a tidal wave right round the world. In Britain the main epidemics were in
1831–2, 1848–9, 1854 and 1867.

The microbes that cause cholera are found in the excreta of patients suffering
from the disease. Because of this it is possible to catch cholera by contact with
someone who has it, or, for example, by using the same lavatory. But the real
danger comes if the microbes find their way into drinking water. Should this happen
they can be carried over a wide area. Pumping sewage into the rivers and then
using river water for drinking made it very easy for the disease to spread.

An attack of cholera is terrifying, for it is sudden and violent. The patient goes
blue: he has cramp, with diarrhoea and vomiting. In those days nearly half the
people who caught the disease died from it. It is difficult to find out how many
cholera killed, but in London alone nearly 7000 died in the 1831–2 epidemic, and
15 000 in the 1848–9 epidemic. But horrible and frightening though cholera
was, there were other diseases that killed far more people.

Smallpox lingered on. Thanks first of all to inoculation, and then to vaccination,
the disease had begun to die out. But early in the nineteenth century the industrial

Cholera · Typhus · Tuberculosis

The Fleet river. The Fleet is a small tributary of the Thames. For much of its length it did duty as an open sewer in London, making life unpleasant for anyone unfortunate enough to live near it. Courtesy of Greater London Council.

towns began to grow, the slums spread and the poor who lived in them were too ignorant, too superstitious and too indifferent to have their children vaccinated: so smallpox found a new lease of life. The towns were never wholly free of it and there were epidemics from time to time.

Typhoid fever was fairly common. Like cholera it travelled along the water supplies, so that bad sanitation helped it to spread. We have already seen how this disease struck Croydon in 1852.

Typhus was a typical disease of the poor. In the first place, it attacks people who are badly fed and not strong enough to resist. Secondly, it is carried by lice, so that dirty families are the ones most likely to suffer. As we saw in Chapter One, this disease was diminishing at the end of the eighteenth century, but again the growth of the industrial towns with their water shortages, and masses of unwashed, underfed inhabitants, gave both lice and typhus another chance. There was also a lot of immigration from Ireland where typhus was common, and many immigrants brought the disease with them.

But without any doubt, the greatest killer disease in the nineteenth century was tuberculosis. It was also called consumption, because the patient grows pale and thin and gradually wastes away – he is consumed.

There was a lot of romantic nonsense talked about this disease. It was fashionable to look tuberculous – white-faced, thin and languid. Lord Byron once said that he wished he had consumption because then the ladies would find him pale, interesting and attractive. There was an idea that there was some link between consumption and genius. The body wasted away and set the spirit free for fine flights of the imagination into poetry and music. These romantics would have been horrified if they had known just what was happening inside the lungs of a tuberculous patient.

The disease is spread by bacilli floating in the air on tiny specks of sputum which have come from the lungs of someone already infected. They attack the lungs of their new victim in various places, and the body tries to check this by building up hard nodules called tubercles. But the bacilli go on with their attack and sooner or later the tubercles become caseous. They are soft and spongy and the patient spits them out in the form of yellow sputum. When the caseous tubercle has gone, there is a cavity left in the lung. Soon after he has reached this stage the patient usually dies.

The person most likely to catch tuberculosis is someone with a hereditary weakness, badly fed, under mental and physical strain, working and living in dirty, stuffy conditions and in contact with someone who already has the disease. As our industrial towns grew, this type of person became more and more common. By 1750 the disease was already doing serious damage and by the first half of the nineteenth century it may have killed one-third of the people who died. Its ravages went on well into the twentieth century and even today we still need to take our precautions with mass radiography and B.C.G. injections.

Doctors and others found it difficult to cope with these diseases because they did not know what caused them. Pasteur did not discover microbes until 1864. Before then, there were indeed a few people who believed that there might be such things as germs, but they were not able to prove this, and the majority of doctors had other ideas. They believed that smell caused disease. We call this the miasmatic theory, a miasma being a poisonous matter floating in the air. Dr Southwood Smith claimed that as an animal could be killed by making it breathe the fumes from concentrated prussic acid, so the poisonous fumes from marshes, sewers, dung-heaps, crowded rooms and graveyards acted in the same way: they infected the air, and people who breathed them often became ill and died. One problem with this theory was that it was hard to explain how different diseases came about. A lot depended, they said, on how concentrated the poison was. If fairly dilute, the patient might escape with a headache; if highly concentrated, he could contract a severe bout of fever, and die quickly. Also, much depended on the resistance of the individual. A story told to illustrate this point was about a church where the mats picked up the smell from the bodies in the vaults. A country girl, visiting the town, helped the pew opener to shake these mats. The pew opener, who did the work regularly and was used to the smell, was unwell just for one day. The girl developed fever, and was dead within the week. Another idea, put forward by Dr Lyon Playfair, was that the disease would be different according to the part of the body the miasma attacked. If it spread to the blood it would cause fever; if it went to the intestines, it could cause dysentery, diarrhoea or even tuberculosis. The season, or the year, mattered. Dr Arnott attended a school which had bad drains: in different years, he said, the same smell caused different diseases — in one year the pupils had convulsions, in another ophthalmia, and in another, typhoid fever.

Miasmatic Theory of Disease

Faraday giving his card to Father Thames. Though not all clear about the true cause of disease, people realised that the Thames was a danger to health, since it took the sewage of most of London and was also used as a source of drinking water. This cartoon was drawn when an exceptionally hot, dry summer made the river unbearably offensive.
Reproduced by permission of *Punch*.

NOTICE!!!

We are credibly informed by a correspondent that the much-admired

JAPANESE CHEROOTS

are highly recommended by the faculty abroad as being a sure preventive of that raging disorder the

Cholera Morbus;

they have been recently imported into this Country, and are found to be of that mild and fragrant nature that they may be used by

The Fair Sex

without producing nausea. Their confirmed anti-contagious virtues and delicate fragrance have already procured them a very high and just estimation.

Vide Morning Herald, Nov. 12, 1831.

ARLISS, Printer, Addle Street, Wood Street, Cheapside.

The cholera scare. Cholera was much dreaded and as no one knew what caused it, charlatans of all kinds had the opportunity to make money from credulous people. How far the man who sold the cheroots believed his own patter it is impossible to say. Courtesy of Guildhall Library, City of London.

Obviously, these ideas were bound to lead people astray. We have already seen how Croydon had a typhoid epidemic because sewage found its way into the water supplies. The Board of Health at once looked for the smell which they thought must be causing the disease; but there was no smell, so they were baffled. It could be the sewer, they agreed, but it could not possibly be the water as that was obviously clean and fresh and they advised the people of Croydon to go on drinking it.

21

Miasmatic Theory of Disease

Something as bad happened in the Bristol Royal Infirmary. The doctors there were convinced that the miasma from sick people would not be so dangerous if it was diluted. They thought it was wrong to have all the fever patients in one ward and so they took the patients, suffering from a highly dangerous disease, and spread them evenly through all the wards in the hospital.

Tuberculosis baffled them. They had strange ideas on how one could develop it. Overwork and worry seemed to play a part, but the most popular idea was that it came from bad air. Edwin Chadwick noted that tailors worked packed together in stuffy rooms. 'In the registered causes of death of 233 persons entered under the general head "tailor" no less than 123 died of disease of the respiratory organs of whom 92 died of consumption.' This led doctors to advise fresh air, which of course was good. It also encouraged wealthy people to live in warmer countries, which may not have helped their complaint, but at least meant that they spent their declining years in a pleasant climate. Unhappily, one treatment for tuberculosis was starvation and bleeding which weakened the patient and hastened his end.

Lack of knowledge made it difficult for the Board of Health to control cholera. Chadwick held firmly to two medical theories, both of them false. First of all he believed that all diseases were basically the same; and, secondly, that disease was carried in the atmosphere when poisoned by foul smells.

Under the threat of an epidemic in 1848, Parliament rushed through the Nuisances Removal Act, known also as the Cholera Act. This was to allow the Board of Health to do its work, and Chadwick at once drafted his regulations. One of the symptoms of cholera is acute diarrhoea, and since he held that all diseases were essentially the same, he believed that if diarrhoea could be checked, cholera would be as well. The Board's regulations warned against vegetables and fruit, while anyone with an attack of diarrhoea was to have drugs that would cause constipation. In a roundabout way, this partly worked. People with constipation did not visit the privies so often, and these were the places where it was only too easy to catch the disease.

But Chadwick's idea that smells cause disease proved a disaster. He made superhuman efforts to bully reluctant local authorities into action, and have the sewers flushed, so that each week 6000 cubic yards of filth were swept into the Thames. This took away many of the foul smells that Chadwick feared, but it gave the cholera a real chance. The organisms of the disease were now in the river in great numbers, and it was from the river that most of the water companies took their supplies. The cholera now spread like wildfire, and by the end of 1849 30 000 people in London had caught it and nearly half of these had died.

But, as a general rule, medical theory did not lead doctors too far astray. The miasmatic theory led to some good results. To be rid of your smells, you must first be rid of your dirt, and if the dirt goes, most germs go with it. Reformers who wanted to clean up the cities were indeed aiming at the right thing.

22

Disease

ORIGINAL SOURCES

Bateman, Thomas. *Report on the Diseases of London*. Longman, Hurst, Rees, Orme and Brown, 1819. This is interesting for its attempt to link the incidence of disease with changes in the atmosphere.

Chadwick, Edwin. *Supplementary Report on the Practice of Interment in Towns*. 1843. In this book Chadwick gives some clear explanations of the miasmatic theory of disease.

Leigh, Rev J. B. *An Authentic Narrative of the Melancholy Occurrences At Bilston, August and September 1832*. 1833. A vivid contemporary account of the cholera outbreak in Bilston, which had the highest death rate per capita of any town in England.

Shapter, Thomas. *The History of Cholera in Exeter*. John Churchill, 1849. A fascinating description of the cholera epidemic in one town, particularly good on the psychological impact of the disease on the community.

Snow, John. *On the Mode of Communication of Cholera*. John Churchill, 1855. Dr Snow describes his detective work in tracking down the causes of cholera.

FURTHER READING

Buer, M. C. *Health, Wealth and Population in the Early Days of the Industrial Revolution*. Routledge, London, 1968.

Dubos, René and Jean. *The White Plague – Tuberculosis, Man and Society*. Gollancz, London, 1953.

Longmate, Norman. *King Cholera*. Hamish Hamilton, London, 1966. This contains a vivid account of the cholera epidemics.

LITERARY SOURCES

Dickens, Charles. *Martin Chuzzlewit*. Penguin, Harmondsworth, 1968. (Chapters 25 and 29: Sarah Gamp.)

Dickens, Charles. *Sketches by Boz*. Everyman's Library, Dent, London, 1968. (Chapter 6: a hospital.)

Dickens, Charles. *The Uncommercial Traveller*. Everyman's Library, Dent, London, 1969. (Chapter 32: a children's hospital.)

Gaskell, Elizabeth. *Mary Barton*. Penguin, Harmondsworth, 1970. (Chapter 6: an attack of typhus and medical treatment.)

4 *Working conditions*

TWO FACTORS AFFECT A MAN'S WORK. IN THE FIRST PLACE HE IS AT THE MERCY OF THE general economic state of the country; this will decide such things as the national level of wages, how much these wages will buy, and the amount of unemployment. Secondly, the working conditions in the man's own trade are important. What hours does this particular trade work? What wages does it pay? Is the work dirty or dangerous? Is anything done to make unpleasant work more bearable?

This chapter will fall into two parts. First of all we shall look at some of the more important economic changes in the country as a whole. Then we shall look at conditions in four specific industries: coal and cotton, which were organised in large units, nail-making which was based on small workshops, and handloom weaving, which was done in the home.

Changes in the economy

There were three kinds of change that took place in the economy of the country. We can call them seasonal, secular and cyclical. All of them had important effects on the ordinary working class family.

Farming is a good example of a seasonal trade. There were times during the year, for example during the harvest, when the whole family helped, and worked for as long as there was daylight; at other times the employers were hard-pressed to find work just for the men. Coal-mining tended to be seasonal, in that there was more demand during the winter, though this was marginal, as domestic consumption only accounted for part of the demand. Building was another seasonal trade for work sometimes stopped and nearly always slowed down during the winter months.

The harvest was another seasonal event which was unpredictable. The labourer and his family lived almost entirely on bread; a bad harvest meant high prices, and this in turn brought hardship. If, along with the high price of bread, there was widespread unemployment, then there was disaster. This happened in 1801, when many men were out of work, and after there had been bad harvests in 1799 and 1800. Not surprisingly, there was much discontent, and some rioting.

Secular trends last for a long time. We can contrast two periods – the first spans the Napoleonic Wars, from 1788 to 1814, while the second was from 1814 to about 1850.

During the war this country spent a great deal of money abroad. Britain had to maintain her own army and navy, and was constantly making loans and grants to prop up tottering allies on the Continent. These loans usually went as goods, which created a shortage and high prices in this country. It is a general rule that wages follow prices: if prices go up, so do wages, but only after a while. The worker realises prices have risen, he claims extra pay, and the employer usually refuses him. There is a dispute, perhaps even a strike, and by the time the worker has won his point, prices have jumped ahead again. If prices rise over a long period, wages gradually lose their purchasing power; money wages may go up, but real wages fall. This is what happened in England during the Napoleonic Wars.

After the war the drain on capital largely stopped. There were a few unwise investments in South American silver mines but for the most part, people invested at home and in very useful enterprises – cotton mills, shipyards, docks, iron works, coal-mines and railways. Production increased, the volume of goods increased, and prices fell. Wages fell too, but once again they followed prices. This time it was the employer who put on the pressure. By the time his workers had agreed to take lower wages, prices had fallen still further, so they were better off in spite of having less money. While money wages fell, 'real' wages rose, so that most workers were more prosperous in 1850 than they had been in 1815.

Finally, we come to the cyclical changes which caused widespread upset to people in all walks of life. During the Industrial Revolution, the British economy expanded more rapidly than ever before, but it was not a smooth expansion. Instead it went forward in a series of sudden bursts of activity, followed by unpleasant set-backs. These movements are called business, or trade, cycles.

A cycle would begin with a growth in foreign trade. Foreigners were willing to pay good prices, and this encouraged the manufacturers to produce more. They employed more people, they worked their factories for longer hours, and they used their machines to capacity. With more and more people in work, manufacturers found that they had to pay higher wages. This is a period of expansion, or a boom. Its marks are:

> rising demand leading to rising prices
> increased production
> rising wages
> a fall in unemployment.

This state of affairs could not go on for ever. In his eagerness to make money, a manufacturer might well push his prices too high for his customers; indeed he might have no choice, because the high wages he was paying would compel him to raise the prices of his goods. Again, he might be over-optimistic about the state of his market and flood it with more goods than it could take. Perhaps because his prices were too high, or because he had produced too many goods, or because of both these things, demand would slacken and the warehouses would begin to fill with unwanted goods. The only thing to do would be to cut back production. The factory would go on short time, and employees would be laid off. To sell his goods the manufacturer would want to cut prices; this meant cutting costs, which in turn meant paying lower wages. As there was now little demand for labour, the workers would have no choice but to take less money. Here we have the opposite of a boom;

25

Changes in the economy

we call it a recession or a slump. Its marks are:

> falling demand leading to falling prices
> falling production
> falling wages
> rising unemployment.

But, like a boom, a recession does not last for ever. The customers wear out their goods, the low prices encourage them to buy, the warehouses empty, and where there has once been plenty, there is once again a shortage. The demand revives, trade and industry revive with it, and a new boom begins.

The length of time for the whole cycle was usually about four years. Every alternate cycle followed a different pattern. It would begin with the revival of foreign trade in just the same way but as the boom went on people would invest the profits they were making in important enterprises in this country. For example, in 1791–3 there was a lot of canal building; in 1824–5 many factories, particularly textile factories, were built; in 1835–6 and again in 1844–5 there was much speculation in railways. Of course, a large boom went far beyond making full use of existing plant; it meant modernizing, expanding, and setting up new concerns. At the height of a boom, there would be full employment and wages would be at their highest. Unfortunately, when the recession did come it was more violent than in one of the minor cycles. Wages fell badly, and there was mass unemployment.

This insistent rhythm of the business cycle continued through much of the eighteenth century, it was a constant problem in the nineteenth, and persisted until the 1930s. Moreover, as time went on, cycles grew in size and importance, so that each recession brought with it more suffering and anxiety.

Obviously this state of affairs was bad for the working man. During a boom he was fairly sure of a job, and fairly sure that his wages would rise. But as the boom reached its peak, the pressure of overwork would perhaps be more than he could bear. After the boom came the recession and with it falling wages, short time, and quite probably, unemployment. These were times of hunger, worry and discontent. As we shall see it was during recessions that the working classes were at their most active in pressing for reforms. It was when they were out of work and hungry that they listened most readily to people like the Chartists (see page 86).

For the ordinary working man the general economic state of the country was not favourable. In any year there might be a bad harvest, which would drive food prices impossibly high, there were seasonal fluctuations, and all the time there was the trade cycle. The only good development was the rise in real wages between 1815 and 1850. In an average year the average worker was somewhat better off at the end of our period, than he had been at the beginning.

We must now look at conditions in some specific industries.

Coal-mining

Mines are unpleasant. They are dark, dirty and can be uncomfortably hot. They are nearly always wet, and indeed, water has always been one of the miner's enemies. In the seventeenth century deep mines were not practicable because they had no pumps effective enough to keep them from flooding. However, in 1710 Newcomen invented his engine and by 1712 mine owners were beginning to use it. It would drain the deepest of mines, but this did not mean that they were dry. Water flowed through the workings into the sump and in places the miners would find themselves wading with water up to their knees.

Coal hewer.
The man is working in a narrow seam and has to lie flat to wield his pick.
For a contemporary description see below.
Courtesy of Mansell Collection.

It could be unpleasant going from the bottom of the pit shaft to the workings, depending on how thick the seams of coal were. Where seams were six feet high, so also were the main roadways and a man could walk upright. But many seams were only four feet high, and some were as low as two feet or eighteen inches. In these narrow passages there was no machinery to haul the coal so women and children harnessed themselves to the tubs and hauled like animals. For the men at the coal face, we have this description by a visitor to a mine in the West Riding of Yorkshire:

> *I have often been shocked in contemplating the hideous and anything but human appearance of these men, who are generally found in a state of bestial nakedness, lying their whole length on the uneven floor, and supporting their heads upon a board or short crutch; or sitting upon one heel balancing their persons by extending the other. Black and filthy as they are in their low, dark, heated and dismal chambers, they look like a race fallen from the common stock. It did not much surprise me to be told that old age came prematurely upon them; indeed the careworn countenances, the grey hair and furrowed brows I met with at that age were sufficient indications of that fact.* (Parliamentary Papers, 1842. Vol. XII, App.: Pt. II, pp. 63–4.)

Coal-mining

The hours of work varied from district to district, and from season to season — there was less work in the summer. More important, the fortunes of the coal-mine were linked with other industries, and the ceaseless, uneasy rhythm of the trade cycle meant periods of overwork, followed by periods of short time and unemployment.

Assuming that the pit was in full production, the working day was a long one. In Derbyshire they reckoned a full day's work was sixteen hours. Twelve hours was only three-quarters of a day, and eight hours was half a day. In some pits, the men were allowed an hour for dinner, but in the Coalbrookdale district of Shropshire, the winding engine did not stop. The workmen took it in turns to have a few minutes break, while they gobbled their food, and their mates did their work for them.

Quite often the miner was the victim of his own folly. Not all pits had the discipline of a modern factory, and men worked when they felt like it. They would do nothing on Monday, and perhaps start work late on Tuesday. This meant that they spent the end of the week working frantically to make up lost time.

In spite of the bad conditions it seems that the miners enjoyed better health than the majority of workers. In a good pit there was always plenty of fresh air, and so far below ground the temperature hardly varied at all. A Wolverhampton doctor said that the colliers were a much healthier race than the men and boys who worked in the workshops and factories. He said:

> The colliers are so healthy that wounds and large gashes are cured with a rapidity quite surprising; compound fractures are cured with scarcely a troublesome symptom. As to formation, the collier, as he walks, rolls along, swinging at the hips as if he were double jointed; the manufacturer creeps along as if his bones were all huddled together. (Parliamentary Papers, 1842, Vol. XV, p. 14.)

We must remember that this doctor is comparing the miners with men in a depressed trade and that despite their good health, they could not expect to live as long as farm workers, still less as long as a professional man or a gentleman.

Assuming that there was work, miners' wages were reasonably high. A lad of seventeen could earn 10s a week, which was more than an adult farm labourer, and hewers could make anything up to 25s or even 30s a week. With his wife and some of his children in employment, the collier did not want for much, as long as trade was good.

But one thing threatened every mine and that was sudden death; there were few mines where the owners took all the precautions they should. They were lucky in Dolcoath:

> The ventilation in Dolcoath is particularly good, and the men are healthier than in most other mines. There are more old miners. Care is taken for the prevention of accidents. 'Our ladders', says one of the witnesses 'are about two fathoms and a half in length, generally with the staves one foot apart. We use oak staves; old ship oak we find the best. We have had no accidents on our footways for a long time.' They have introduced the safety fuse and the witness says, 'Very few accidents now arise from explosions; they used to happen frequently.' (Edwin Chadwick, op. cit., p. 262.)

But there was no law to compel safety precautions, and in mines where neither owners nor men took care, accidents were common.

The most spectacular accidents were the explosions. These became more and more common as pits became deeper. They were generally caused by methane gas, known to the miners as 'fire damp'. Where pits were well ventilated this gas could not gather in enough quantity to be dangerous, but too many pits, especially the smaller ones, did not have good ventilation. In 1815 Humphrey Davy invented the safety lamp but many mine owners did not give these lamps to their men. Moreover, the men were not always sensible in their use of the lamps. One visitor was horrified to see a group of miners, in a dangerous part of the mine, unscrewing their lamps to trim the wicks.

It was dangerous going up and down the pit shaft, for the winding gear was often primitive. The most crude was the windlass, which was just like the gear found at the top of a well. Whoever was coming up the shaft was quite at the mercy of the winder, for if he jerked he could set his load swinging, or if his attention wandered, he could draw his passengers over the windlass, and send them hurtling back down the shaft. Things were not much better where there was a horse gin, because they often used old, broken-down horses, who jerked the machinery and set the load swinging. Where a steam engine did the winding, there were usually guide rods. These ran from top to bottom of the shaft, passing through eyes on the clatch harness, and this meant that the load could not swing. But there was still the danger of going over the pulley. A rag would be tied to the rope, about sixty feet above the bucket, and when the engine boy saw this, he knew it was time to slow down. The trouble was that he did not always see the rag.

These shafts themselves were dangerous as they were not always properly boarded or bricked. A stone could easily fall out of the side and hit someone down below. The workings were dangerous, too. Usually there were good supports in the permanent roadways, but the side galleries running along the coal face were only temporary and the miners took less care to support the roof. Roof-falls were the most common cause of death.

This was the main problem in mining – the miner's life was at risk from the moment he left the surface to begin his journey into the pit.

Cotton factories

The cotton industry holds a special place in industrial history in that it was the first to develop along modern lines. In the early eighteenth century it was a fairly new industry, so it was not hampered by all the petty restrictions that the older industries had inherited from earlier times. Cotton manufacturers had to fight a running battle with wool manufacturers and they ran into labour troubles, but on the whole they were more free than most to concentrate their work force in factories, to introduce new machinery, to increase output by intelligent organisation, and to build up large business empires. In the early nineteenth century cotton was our leading industry.

Because of its importance, the cotton industry attracted a good deal of notice. It was big, it was obvious, and if there was going to be any state regulation of

Cotton factories

industry, cotton would be the easiest to control. The industry was under attack from philanthropists like Lord Shaftesbury and agitators like Richard Oastler. Even some cotton manufacturers, like Sir Robert Peel the elder, Robert Owen and John Fielden attacked their own kind. In those days the agricultural interest ruled the country, and their concern was to keep wheat prices high which they attempted to do through the Corn Laws. The factory owners on the other hand favoured cheap food so that they could pay low wages. This is one of the reasons why they attacked the Corn Laws, and, not surprisingly, their rivals hit back by supporting the philanthropists in their attempts to secure a ten-hour day, and check the abuse of child labour.

There was a lot of controversy. A number of Parliamentary Committees investigated the industry, some in favour of the employers, some in favour of the workers. There was a spate of pamphlets and books, some attempting to whitewash the industry and show that conditions were ideal, others to show that life in the cotton mills was as near as possible to a hell on earth. What were the facts?

Without a doubt there were bad mills. This is a description of a spinning mill in Kincardineshire:

> It is dirty, unroofed, ill-ventilated, with machinery not boxed in, and passages so narrow that they could hardly be defined; it seemed more to be a receptacle of demons than the workhouse of industrious human beings. The appearance and language of the workers, both men and women, proved the state of demoralisation which exists here. The house of Gilchrist the mill-owner, presented a picture of filth and want of comfort of every kind, such as I have rarely seen elswehere. It was painful to find in the bothy, the eating and sleeping room of such a nest of profligates, two or three young females without a parent or relation in the neighbourhood to look after their conduct, or to make any attempt to rescue them. (Parliamentary Papers, 1833, Vol. XX, A138.)

Some mills were dusty. In all rooms there were minute particles of cotton in the air, called 'fly', but the worst place for this was the scutching room, where they opened the bales of cotton and prepared it for the machines. One witness said that when he went into a scutching room the dust was so thick that he could hardly see the women at work on the machine.

Temperatures could be trying; much depended on the work being done. For ordinary spinning, it was possible to have a comfortable working temperature of 60°F but for fine spinning they needed 70°F. One workman complained that in his weaving shed they needed a temperature of between 85°F and 90°F and that he had often seen the thermometer at 92°F.

Ventilation varied from mill to mill. In the larger ones it can never have been too bad as machines took up most of the floor, and people did not work on top of one another. If the air did become close, it was often the fault of the work-people rather than the factory building. Many of them, being underfed and badly clothed, had a dread of cold air, and would not open the windows.

There were no safety regulations for the mills, and employers did not always box off working parts. Driving belts were dangerous, especially those which had a buckle to adjust them. The shaft which gave the power ran along under the ceiling, and it had drums on it at intervals. The belts which drove the machines ran down from these drums. A woman or girl who did not pay attention could catch her clothes or her hair in the buckle and be flung over the driving shaft. There was no compensation. A poor worker would find it impossible to sue an employer, and all he or she could do was hope for charity. Often workmates would club together to help an injured friend, and quite often the employer would pay something. But he was by no means bound to do this, and many a worker was injured as a result of his employer's negligence and just dismissed.

There were mills, then, that were dirty, dusty, ill-ventilated and dangerous. But there were others that were, for their day and age, model factories. The most famous were the New Lanark Mills, the property of the philanthropist, Robert Owen, and Titus Salt's mills at Saltaire. These mills have been described in many books before and so here is a description of Archibald Buchanan's works at Catrine:

> I had great pleasure in walking through the eighteen apartments of the spinning mills, and power loom weaving establishment, and witnessing the admirable order of the works, and the apparent happiness of the people employed, which is quite remarkable and as obvious as at any of the other great factories situated in country districts. No artificial heat is required, except in the dressing room of the power loom weaving mill; the windows open from the top; the rooms are thoroughly ventilated; there is a clock and a thermometer in every room; no unpleasant smell in any part of the work, and the utmost cleanness and neatness prevailing throughout.
>
> The works are well provided with fanners in the preparing rooms; but the inconvenience arising from the dust of the cotton has not been everywhere so thoroughly removed as in part of the new mill of Deanstown.
>
> There are between 800 and 900 workers all occupying houses originally built by the company, of a very different and superior description from those generally occupied by persons of the same situation in life in this country. They have a chapel, and every establishment necessary for their accommodation.
>
> Although we were only a few hours at Catrine, we saw enough to satisfy us of the high estimation in which Mr Buchanan is held by the community which he superintends. (Ibid., AI 93.)

But however good the mills were, the hours were likely to vary. No trade was as subject as cotton to the trade cycle. When trade was bad, there would be months of enforced idleness, with short time and unemployment; when trade was good there were frantic periods of overwork. A lad of seventeen from Leicester described his working week in a new factory, built and opened at the height of the boom in 1825. He began at six on Monday and worked right through until eleven at night on Tuesday. He began again at six on Wednesday, and worked through the night and the next day again until eleven on Thursday. On Friday he began again at six and worked through until seven or eight on Saturday evening. He ate his meals while watching his machine, so that his total working week was something like 120 hours. This continued until one day he went to sleep and fell into his machine. He escaped unhurt, but decided the time had come to give up his job.

The nail-makers of Sedgley

The nail-makers of Sedgley

While there are a lot of books and pamphlets about the cotton mills, there is little enough, outside the official reports, on the smaller workshops. People began to investigate these more thoroughly in the later part of the nineteenth century, but the evil had been there for some time. The workshops of the nail-makers of Sedgley were typical. These little dens were small, badly built, badly ventilated, and surrounded by dirt, filth, and refuse of all kinds. Their floors were usually below ground level and the only way to clean them was to shovel the rubbish into the street. When their forges were out these places looked like neglected coal holes. With the forges lit and the people at work the fumes and the noise were overpowering. A whole family would be crowded into a room about ten feet square, so close together that they had to climb over one another if they wanted to come in or go out.

All day long they did nothing but hammer. The local factor gave them iron rods which they made into nails. First of all the worker took a red hot rod and beat it so that it tapered. This made the point and at the same time separated the nail from the end of the rod. He then held it upright in a pair of pincers and flattened the end to make the head. They made a great many nails in a day; even a child was supposed to make 1000.

There was a good deal written about the evils of the large factories, but it needs only a little imagination to realise that the factory was an improvement on the miserable little dens which the working men provided for their own use.

The handloom weavers

The story of the handloom weavers shows what life was like for craftsmen who did not change their methods with the times. The Industrial Revolution made its first big strides after the end of the war with France. We have already seen what the secular trends were in this period between 1815 and 1850. Prices fell and in order to go on making good profits, manufacturers expanded production by using new machines, building bigger factories and streamlining their organisation. Greater efficiency brought benefits in a plentiful supply of cheap goods such as there had never been before. Manufacturers did well: their profits on any single item fell, but they produced so many more goods that they made large sums of money. Workers in the expanding industries like cotton, coal-mining and iron also did well. Their wages dropped, but not so fast as the cost of living, so, as we have seen, they were more prosperous in 1850 than they had been in 1815.

But there were people who had no share in this success. What if a man finds that prices are falling, but has no way of improving his techniques to expand production? All he can do is to work longer and longer hours for less and less money, until his life becomes one of ceaseless, unrewarding toil. This happened to a good many craftsmen after 1815, but those who attracted most attention were the handloom weavers.

In the late eighteenth century the weavers had prospered. Kay's 'flying shuttle' meant that they could double their output, and the invention of the 'spinning jenny', the 'water frame' and the 'mule' meant they could have all the thread they needed. Weavers were in demand. They asked for high wages and they got them.

The handloom weavers

It was a pleasant life, too, in that the weaver worked at home and chose his own hours. If he felt like stopping work to potter in his garden, or have a mug of beer with a friend, then he could do so. If he chose to have Monday off and most of Tuesday, that was his own affair; with a little exertion he could earn enough during the rest of the week to keep himself and his family in comfort. But by the end of the eighteenth century, this golden age was over. These are the wages paid during different years for weaving a length of cambric.

1795	33s 3d	1815	14s
1800	25s	1820	9s
1805	25s	1825	8s 6d
1810	19s 6d	1830	5s 6d

In 1830 a man had to work six times as long to make the same money as he had earned in 1795. There were several reasons for this. In the first place, plain weaving is not difficult to learn. It had been so easy to make money at this trade that far more people took it up than could hope to find full-time work at it. English weavers complained bitterly of the Irish immigrants who came to this country, already used to a low standard of living and content with a small wage for long hours of work. Of course, the masters took advantage of the good supply of labour to lower wages.

Then competition came from the power looms. Cartwright invented this machine in 1785, but it was some time before it came into general use. When it did, it meant the doom of the handloom weavers. One of them complained:

> I conceive the evils of machinery to handloom weavers to be very great. It is production without consumption. The work is done by fire and water and brought into the market cheaper than human power can do it. For the benefit of society there ought to be a tax upon it, to enable human labour to compete with it. (Parliamentary Papers, 1840, Vol. XXIII, p. 590.)

But the manufacturers had other ideas. Cloth made on the power looms was woven more evenly than that on handlooms and commanded a better price. Also, when he took an order, a manufacturer was able to say definitely when it would be ready, something he could not do if he relied on the uncertain services of handloom weavers. Moreover, since the work was done in his own factory, he could be sure that no one was going to embezzle his thread.

The handloom weavers clung obstinately to their antiquated machinery, and while factory workers made good wages, they slaved for hours for a few shillings a week in order to keep their independence. But the economic pressures were too strong for them in the end and they were squeezed out of existence.

The handloom weavers were not alone. The same thing happened to the button-makers of Dorset, the lacemakers of Wiltshire, and in time, to the stocking-weavers of Leicestershire. Everywhere that the old domestic crafts felt the cold wind of progress there was the same agonising choice — either the worker fought a slow, miserable, losing battle with economic forces too strong for him, or else he swallowed his pride and submitted to the discipline of the factory.

Factory reform

Tailor's workshop. The man and his wife are working and making their children work under conditions much worse than would be found in most factories. Parliament was willing to begin the regulation of cotton factories as early as 1802, but it was late in the nineteenth century before anything was done about small workshops. Courtesy of Guildhall Library, City of London.

During our period, little was done to check all these evils. The government did not have either the power or the knowledge to tame the trade cycle, and it is only since the Second World War that progress has been made. Bad conditions in the workshops, mines and factories remained, the only important reform being the reduction of the working day in textile mills to a maximum of ten hours. Even here it was useless to ask Parliament to protect adults against overwork. Many people firmly believed that there should be as few restrictions on freedom as possible and that if an adult chose to work himself to death, then he had a perfect right to do so.

To gain any advantage at all the reformers had to concentrate on protecting children. Children are not free to run their own lives and it was possible, although with some difficulty, to persuade Parliament to pass laws protecting them. However, in those days adults and children worked so closely together that the adults could not manage alone, and limiting the hours of children meant, in practice, limiting the hours of adults. By 1850 the ten-hour day was the rule in the textile factories, but the story of how this came about really belongs to the next chapter.

ORIGINAL SOURCES

Leifchild, J. R. *Our Coal Fields and Coal Pits.* Library of Industrial Classics, Cass, London, 1968.

Pike, E. Royston. *Human Documents of the Industrial Revolution.* Allen and Unwin, London, 1966.

Taylor, W. Cook. *Notes of a Tour in the Manufacturing Districts of Lancashire in 1842.* An account of life in the cotton towns during a depression.

FURTHER READING

Fitton, R. S. and Wadsworth, A. P. *The Strutts and the Arkwrights 1758–1830*. Manchester University Press, Manchester, 1958.
Hammond, J. L. and Hammond, Barbara. *Skilled Labourer*. Longman, London, 1919.

LITERARY SOURCES

Gaskell, Elizabeth. *Mary Barton*. Penguin, Harmondsworth, 1970. (Chapter 1: appearance of factory workers; chapters 3, 8 and 11: effects of trade depression and unemployment.)
Gaskell, Elizabeth. *North and South*. Penguin, Harmondsworth, 1970. (Chapter 13: lung disease caught in a cotton factory.)
Kingsley, Charles. *Alton Locke*. Everyman's Library, Dent, London, 1970. (Chapter 2: tailor's workroom; chapter 8: sweated labour.)

5 Child labour

Children have always had work to do and this is as it should be, provided what they do is good for them. Only too often during the Industrial Revolution it was not. We will see what happened in a number of industries.

Cotton

Cotton manufacturers could say that few children in their factories did heavy work. Most of the youngest ones were scavengers who had to pick loose cotton from the floor and piecers who had to join threads together in the spinning machines. Certainly neither job was hard. The economist, Nassau Senior, who supported the factory system, claimed that there was less to do than in a shop. He said he had seen factory girls standing with their arms folded, while others were sewing or sitting down.

But this was not the whole truth. There was a kindly manufacturer called John Fielden, who was a good friend to working people and ran his factory in as humane a way as he knew. He was also Member of Parliament for Oldham and one day he and some other M.P.s met a deputation of working people at Manchester. This is what happened:

> One of these delegates gave a statement with particulars of a calculation of the number of miles which a child had to walk in a day in minding the spinning machine; it amounted to twenty-five! The statement excited great surprise: but this delegate was followed by another who had also made calculations. He calculated that a child has to walk twenty-four miles in the day: and, if the distance that it frequently has to walk to and from home be thrown in, it makes, not infrequently, a distance of nearly thirty miles. (John Fielden, *The Curse of the Factory System*.)

Fielden investigated his own factory and found to his dismay that children there were walking nearly as far. This is how a boy of seven, Robert Blincoe, found his first day in a factory:

> They reached the mill about half-past five. Blincoe heard a burring sound before he reached the portals, and smelt the fumes of the oil with which the axles of twenty-thousand wheels and spindles were bathed. The moment he entered the doors, the noise appalled him, and the stench seemed intolerable.

> *The task first allotted to him was to pick up the loose cotton that fell upon the floor. Apparently nothing could be easier, and he set to with diligence, although much terrified by the whirling motion and noise of the machinery, and not a little affected by the dust and flue with which he was half suffocated. Unused to the stench he soon felt sick, and by constantly stooping, his back ached. Blincoe therefore took the liberty to sit down: but this attitude, he soon found, was strictly forbidden. His task-master gave him to understand he must keep on his legs. He did so, till twelve o'clock, being six hours and a half without the least intermission. Blincoe suffered greatly with thirst and hunger.* (John Brown, *A Memoir of Robert Blincoe*, p. 15.)

At twelve o'clock, this little boy had only finished half his work for the day.

We learned in the last chapter how work in the cotton mills sometimes went on for more hours than an adult could stand. But children had to help the adults, and although it may well have been true that their work was quite light, the fact that it went on for so long made it intolerable.

Coal mines

Coal mines were even more unpleasant than factories. The youngest children were trappers. At various places in the mines there were doors that had to stay shut most of the time so that air would circulate to all the workings. A trapper sat at each of these doors and pulled it open with a piece of string every time a load of coal came by. A member of the Royal Commission that looked into the problem of child labour in the mines found the following:

> *The children that excite the greatest pity are those who stand behind the doors to open and shut them: they are called trappers, who in the darkness, solitude and stillness as of night, eke out a miserable existence for the smallest of wages. I can never forget the first unfortunate creature that I met with: it was a boy of about eight years old, who looked at me as I passed with an expression the most abject and idiotic – like a thing, a creeping thing, peculiar to the place. On approaching and speaking to him he shrank trembling and frightened into a corner.* (Parliamentary Papers, 1842, Vol. XV, p. 72.)

Many trappers worked in darkness. Their parents would give them enough candle to go to and from their place of work, and that was all. It was quite unusual for there to be any pit lights nearby. As to the company he had, this was not likely to cheer him much. He was more likely to receive a curse or a blow for being slow to open his door than a kind word. Sometimes a miner would tell the little boy that hobgoblins were coming and then go away and leave him alone with his imagination and the darkness. The only comfort was that the trappers' work was not hard. They could at least do it without too much physical strain.

Older children, called hurriers, brought coal from the face to the foot of the shaft. They had to drag the loaded tubs of coal, called corves, which, fully loaded, could weigh anything from two to five hundredweight. The coal hewers were paid according to the amount of coal they sent up to the surface, so if their hurriers let them

Coal mines

Girl coal bearers in East Scotland. In some of the smaller mines coal was carried to the surface in this way. Each girl had a flat basket called a creel, and it was held in place by a strap called a tug, that went round her forehead. Sometimes a tug would break as is shown in the picture. A girl might carry over a hundredweight of coal at a time, and it was calculated that in one pit the distance walked and climbed was equal to the height of St Paul's. The children worked for their fathers who dug the coal and then loaded them in this way. Courtesy of Radio Times Hulton Picture Library.

down they lost money. If a hurrier wasted time he could expect no mercy from his hewer. Not only was the work hard, but the children had to keep at it – they were not called hurriers for nothing!

Metal trades in South Staffordshire

All sorts of metal goods were made in south Staffordshire. We shall look at the locksmiths of Wolverhampton and Willenhall.

Lock-making was complicated, but the work was divided into so many simple processes that it was not at all interesting. Some lock parts were forged, others stamped out in a press, and others filed to shape. Filing, the most common job of all, was very dull. A soon as a child had enough strength he was put to work, standing on a block so that he could reach the vice. Here he stayed by the hour, without changing his position or his action, filing little bits of iron into shape.

This is how a visitor to Wolverhampton described the places where they had to work:

> *Of the great mass of little workshops, of whatevever kind, but particularly of the keymakers and locksmiths, they have one common characteristic, viz. want of open space in the shop; want of ventilation; and the shop itself is situated in some very close and dirty locality at the back of squalid houses, and in the vicinity of, if not facing, some filthy accumulations . . . Many of the shops are extremely dirty and dilapidated, sometimes presenting the appearance of little broken sheds. Their floor is generally the earth, a few are boarded, many are bricks. Their windows are often a mere hole in the wall, into which a shutter is fitted at night. They must be wretched places in winter, especially for the feet of those who stand from day to day at the vice.* (Ibid., Pt. II, q. 44.)

Hours

One of the most active reformers of the early nineteenth century was Robert Owen, the mill owner. He took no children below the age of ten, and they worked ten and three-quarter hours a day, not counting meals. This, he told a Royal Commission, was too long. When asked what hours he would recommend, he said ten hours would be enough, or at the most, ten and a half. Owen was a kindly employer but many other mill-owners were not so considerate. At Blackbarrow Mill in Lancashire children started at five in the morning. They had half an hour for breakfast at seven o'clock; they then worked until noon, when they had another half an hour off for dinner. They had tea later on, but had to eat it while they worked. Their labours would not normally finish before eight. This meant a fifteen-hour day, fourteen hours of which were work.

In other industries we find the same sad story. The girl coal bearers in Scotland worked for twelve, fourteen or sixteen hours and so did the children in the metal trades around Birmingham. In normal times, with the mills and workshops in full production, a child was lucky to escape with twelve hours work a day. He was more than fortunate if he worked for Robert Owen, or someone like him, who asked for less than eleven hours.

In some industries not only were there too many working hours in the week, but the time would be badly distributed. The most common reason for this was the irregular habits of the grown-up workmen. Not all factories worked by the bell, so that workers could come in and out as they pleased. Where people worked at home they could suit themselves entirely. It was quite common to have Monday off, and do only a little work on Tuesday. On Wednesday they might do a fair day's work, but by Thursday they would be in a panic. This is what the end of the week was like in Wolverhampton:

> *Lights are seen in the shops of many of the small masters as late as ten or eleven o'clock on Thursday.*

Hours ·Wages

During the whole of Friday the town is silent in all the main streets and thorough-fares, and seems to have been depopulated of all its manufacturers. Lights appear in the workshops to a late hour in the night – sometimes till morning.

All Saturday morning the streets present the same comparatively barren and silent appearance. Everybody is working for his life. Among the small masters their wives, children and apprentices are being almost worked to death.

Kicks, cuffs, curses and blows are abundantly administered to the children at this crisis of the week. (Ibid., q. 24.)

We must, however, bear in mind that we have been looking at conditions when mines, factories and workshops were at full production. If we were to believe many of the emotional pamphlets of the period about child labour, and even many of the official reports, we would imagine there was no such thing as short time. But all trades were subject to fluctuations, the cotton trade particularly. For every boom during which the mills worked flat out, there would be a depression when they would have little work to do. Parliament passed the Ten Hours Act at a time when most factories were not working nearly as long as ten hours a day, and some had stopped work altogether.

Wages

Wages were different in different jobs but, wherever they worked, children earned little enough for all their hours of dull, hard work.

Market for hiring children. The services of pauper children are being offered to any workman or tradesmen who wants them. Courtesy of Mansell Collection.

One of the worst-paid jobs was pin-making. Here a child might earn only 1s 6d a week up to the age of thirteen and the average was only 2s 6d. This would hardly buy enough bread and potatoes to feed him, so only the very poorest would do the work. In one of the pin factories there were two motherless children who earned between them 4s or 5s a week. As they had no one to feed them, the overlooker used to cook potatoes for their dinners and take the money out of their wages. Sometimes the cost of the potatoes was as much as their wages, and they had no money to take home at the weekend.

Wages were a little better in the cotton factories, but children under nine might only earn 1s 6d while 4s was considered a fair wage for a lad of eleven.

One of the best paid jobs for children, as well as adults, was coal-mining, but as this table shows, pay was not generous:

Average Wages in Coal-mines, Bradford and Leeds 1842

Age of child	Wage
5	2s 6d
6	2s 6d
7	2s 8d
8	3s
9	3s 5d
10	4s
11	4s 7d
12	5s 4d
13	6s 4d
14	7s 2d
15	7s 10d
16	8s 7d
17	10s 3d

In one way it made little difference to a child whether he earned much or little. He would have to give all his money to his parents and hope that they would allow him a penny or two for pocket-money. Parents used their children to make money – sometimes because they were greedy, and sometimes because they had to. You can see how important children's earnings could be from this weekly budget of a handloom weaver, at Elland in 1842:

Earnings		Expenses	
Father, weaver	10s	Rent	1s 6d
Wife, winder	2s	Coal	1s 6d
Boy, 14, piecer	4s	Food	10s 9½d
Boy, 10, piecer	3s	Misc. (soaps, etc.)	1s 3½d
	19s		15s 1d

S.P.O.T.I.R.—D

Cruelty

This left the family a balance of 3s 11d for clothing and other expenses, but without the earnings of the two boys they would have been unable to meet their basic needs of food, warmth and shelter.

Cruelty

The usual way to ill-treat a child was to beat him. In a factory an overlooker would keep a strap specially for this, otherwise he could use anything that was handy – a piece of the machinery, a stick from the garden, or his bare fist. The Chief Constable of Oldham described how the miners used to give a beating. One of them would hold the boy's head between his knees while the others came along and each gave him several strokes on the bare bottom with a piece of wood. The beating would leave the boy unable to work for several days.

One of the most cruel practices was common among the nail-makers of Sedgley. When a bar of white-hot iron comes out of the furnace it is covered with hundreds of tiny particles. Usually the workman would shake them to the ground, but if he wanted to punish a child he would shower the sparks all over him. They called this sending a 'flash of lightning'.

There were many reasons for the cruelty. Then, as now, children misbehaved and needed to be punished. Reasonable punishment is not cruelty, but too much of this so-called punishment was, as it went far beyond what was necessary to reprimand a child.

One complaint was that children spoilt their work. They would not pay proper attention to their machine and something would go wrong; sometimes they would fall asleep. But in view of the hours they worked it is not surprising that their minds wandered or that they could not keep awake. During the last dark hours of a long winter's day, only savage treatment could keep a child awake and concentrating.

Another reason is that in a large factory or mine, the man who employed the children was not the owner, but the adult workman. For example, in the Derbyshire mines, it was reported that 'the treatment of the Children is left entirely to the butty, or the overlooker, who bargains for, dismisses and uses the Child just as he pleases'.

The factory and mine owners did little to protect the children, and in fact, they were the real cause of the trouble. They did not usually ill-treat children themselves, but they were responsible for the system that encouraged ignorant workmen to be cruel.

It could be worse to work for a small master than to be in a factory. Most of them were as uncivilised as ordinary workmen and they had other problems as well. Often they were very poor, like the locksmiths of Wolverhampton. These could barely earn enough to keep themselves, and the worry irritated them and made them cruel. As they were half-starved and badly clothed themselves, it was not surprising that their young workers were as well.

A general problem was the lack of good standards of treatment. Too many people just did not know what it was to lead a decent life. The Commissioner who reported on the state of the child workers of Wolverhampton wrote:

I would draw your attention to the passive and uncomplaining nature of the evidence taken from so many children and young persons in painful circumstances. I cannot but consider this in itself as evidence of their low and depressed condition – the poverty of their spiritual and moral nature. Many of these poor children deposing that they worked from twelve to fourteen hours a day for 1s 6d or 2s 6d a week, not a penny of which they had for their own use, and often without any regular hours for their meals; who were clothed in rags: who acknowledged that they felt often sick or otherwise ill, and that they had not enough to eat – who were some-times 'beaten badly', but who 'only felt it for a day or two' – have still replied that they 'liked their work', 'were well-treated', 'were only punished when they deserved it', etc. They evidently knew of nothing else but to wake and go to work from day to day, and to continue working until permitted to leave off. Such a question as 'Do you feel tired?' had never before been asked them, and they did not understand it. (Ibid., q. 2.)

Children treated like this were unlikely to grow up into kindly employers.

Age of child workers

Together with the long hours, the early age at which children began work was one of the worst features of child labour. The Royal Commission of 1833 summed up the position in factories:

In some rare instances children begin to work in factories at five years old: it is not uncommon to find them there at six; many are under seven: still more under eight: but the greater number are nine: while some, but comparatively few, branches of manufacture do not admit of the employment of children under ten years of age. (Parliamentary Papers, 1833, Vol. XX, p. 19.)

It was the same in the mines. This story comes from the Report of 1842.

There is evidence that some children begin work in the pits of the Coalbrook Dale district as early as six years of age. One instance indeed came under the observation of the sub-Commissioner, in which a child two years younger, that is four years of age, was regularly taken into the pit by his father. 'This remarkable instance became known to me,' says Dr Mitchell, 'when exploring the Hills Lane Pit, the ground-bailiff and a labouring collier accompanied me.' 'I say, Jones,' said the ground-bailiff to one of the charter-masters, 'there are very few children working in this mine: I think we have none under ten or eleven.' The collier immediately said, 'Sir, my little boy is only a little more than four.' This was a very unseasonable interruption and all the ground-bailiff said was, 'Well, I suppose you take good care of him: you take him down and up when you go yourself.' (Parliamentary Papers, 1842, Vol. XV, p. 9.)

The children who were worst off were those who worked for their parents at home. The stocking-weavers of Leicestershire put their children to work as soon as they could handle a needle, and this was at the age of three.

Apprentices

The reason children started work so young was usually that their parents were unable to support the family by themselves. Also, the coming of machinery created many easy jobs which children could do for small wages. The factory owners therefore saw no reason to employ adults for higher wages.

Apprentices

Apprenticeship began in the Middle Ages. It grew in importance and in 1562 Parliament passed the Statute of Artificers which made it compulsory for all boys who wanted to enter a skilled trade. Apprenticeship worked quite well as a system of industrial training until the eighteenth century, but as industry began to develop, employers lost patience with it. They wanted to employ large numbers of workmen, not just a handful of apprentices. Apprenticeship gradually declined until 1814 when Parliament repealed the Statute of Artificers.

But there was another kind of apprentice – one who was not learning a skilled trade. This was the pauper apprentice. Where a child was in the care of the parish, the poor law authorities had the right to bind him apprentice with a local tradesman. There is a vivid description of how this happened in *Oliver Twist*. The employer had a small premium from the parish and promised to feed, clothe and look after the child. In return the child had to work for the master without wages until the age of twenty-one. So far the two systems are alike, but the important difference was that the master had no duty to teach the pauper a trade. He could use him to do housework, run errands or do any job however unskilled or unpleasant it might be. When the child was twenty-one and the so-called apprenticeship was over, he had probably learnt nothing and was fit only for unskilled labour. Towards the end of the eighteenth century, while skilled apprentices were becoming rarer, pauper apprentices were suddenly in high demand.

It began in the cotton industry. Many of the new machines needed water-power and so factories had to be built where it was convenient to have dams, and where fast-flowing streams would keep the dams full. Too often this was in remote valleys, away from towns and villages, and the factory owners could not persuade people to go and live out in the wilds. But much of the factory work was so simple that children could do it, so the owners built apprentice houses and then applied to the poor law authorities in the cities for pauper children to fill them. This was an opportunity to empty the workhouses and save the ratepayers' money. The poor law authorities packed the children off to the factories, only too glad to be rid of them, and cared little or nothing what became of them.

This horrible trade in pauper children came to an end in the cotton mills before long. It was not that employers had a change of heart or that Parliament forbade it. What happened was that the textile industries went over from water power to steam and this meant that the factories could move in from the remote valleys to the towns. Here there was no shortage of 'free' children, whose parents were only too eager to send them into the mills.

Results

Hard work and bad treatment made the working children unhealthy. Dr Dutton gave evidence before the 1816 Commission; he said that in the mills he had visited the children were suffering badly from overwork and many of them had crooked legs from standing for so long. The cotton dust, or fly, inflamed their lungs and intestines and was one of the reasons, he said, why they caught scrofula. Dr Southwood Smith claimed he had discovered a 'spinners pthisis' also brought on by the cotton dust. Scrofula and pthisis are both names for different kinds of tuberculosis, and it is quite certain that no one caught this disease from cotton dust. But tuberculosis thrives best in undernourished, overworked bodies, so indirectly the work in the mills helped to spread the disease. The crooked limbs were nearly as much the result of bad feeding as of standing for long hours, but the mills were largely responsible. The common people could not join in the medical arguments, but they knew only too well that their feet swelled, that their legs and hips ached, that they were often hoarse from coughing, and that they grew up neither tall nor straight.

Oddly enough, as we found in Chapter Four, coal-mining seems to have been relatively healthy. The temperature was even all the year round, and in the good pits there was a steady current of fresh air passing through. A young hurrier would be small for his age, and he might be bald on the top of the head from pushing his corve, but he would be muscular, and he would not have any serious disease. His great danger was being injured, but his wounds would heal quickly – a sure sign of good health. Also, as mining was a reasonably well-paid job, many colliers ate well.

The children who had the worst health seem to have been those in the south Staffordshire metal trades. The Report of 1842 describes the children of Wolverhampton:

> *They are stunted in height, meagre in size, their complexions sallow or sickly. The eye is dull; the mouth inexpressive and purposeless. The countenance, generally, is without expression; or if it has any, it is usually either that of hopeless endurance, or of dissatisfaction growing into viciousness. The latter expression was observable in those boys who were stout and healthy, and were shamefully maltreated. The great majority had evidently sunk into a state of passive endurance as though they felt their state and their grievances quite beyond the pale of hope and redress.*
>
> *Many boys are ruptured, some from infancy.*
>
> *A great many showed signs of incipient malformation in the legs and right shoulder.* (Ibid. q. 49.)

As the Report says, rupture and malformation of the limbs were only too common. The local truss-maker had made a fortune, and it was unusual to find a native of the town who was not deformed in one way or another.

But what we must bear in mind is that most children who died did so before they were three – long before they went anywhere near a factory. Also, many of those who grew up were weak and sickly and should never have gone to work. But their parents sent them and, when they died as a result, the factory had simply finished off the evil that had been started so thoroughly in the home.

There were far-reaching results, too, for the country as a whole. Many people in the nineteenth century took quite the wrong view of child labour. Parents looked on children as a source of wages, while employers looked on them as a source of profit. Adults of all kinds used children for their own gain. The children learnt nothing that was of much value to them and, only too often, when they grew up they were turned away from the factories and workshops where their young lives had been squandered. They were members of a vast army of unskilled labourers, who found it nearly impossible to make a decent living for themselves – who in fact, did not even know what decent living was.

Parliament and child labour

At the end of the eighteenth century some people were already worried about the factory children. One of these was Sir Robert Peel, father of the great Sir Robert who became Prime Minister. Peel the elder owned a factory himself so he knew only too well what was happening. In 1802 he persuaded Parliament to pass the Health and Morals of Apprentices Act. Employers were to keep their factories clean by lime-washing the walls every year; they had to call in a doctor at their own expense if there was an outbreak of infectious disease in their factory. They had to give each apprentice a new suit of clothes every year and apprentices had to have lessons – reading, writing and arithmetic during the week, and religion on Sunday. Most important of all, no apprentice was to work more than twelve hours a day.

So far the Act was good, but who was to see that the mill-owners obeyed it? The Act said that the Justices of the Peace in each area should appoint two visitors – one of them was to be himself a J.P. and the other a clergyman. These two were to go round the factories and prosecute any mill-owner who was disobeying the law. Such an arrangement was almost useless since in the factory districts most J.P.s were either mill-owners or the friends of mill-owners. Also Justices had so many jobs that it was impossible to do them all or even to know what they all were. In some places they had not even heard of Peel's Act! The new law can have made hardly any difference to the apprentice children. Employers who had been ill-treating them went on doing so. But Peel's Act was important in one way. It showed that Parliament was willing to interfere with factories, and at least try to stop some of the worst evils found in them.

In the early years of the nineteenth century there was an important movement in the textile districts to shorten the working day which we call the Ten Hours Movement. One of its founders was an estate bailiff called Richard Oastler, who sent a famous letter to the *Leeds Mercury*, entitled 'Yorkshire Slavery'. Oastler wrote it at a time when there was agitation for the abolition of slavery in the British Empire. This is a paragraph from the letter:

> *The very streets which receive the droppings of an Anti-Slavery Society, are every morning wet by the tears of innocent victims at the accursed shrine of avarice, who are compelled, (not by the cart-whip of the negro slave driver) but by the dread of the thong or strap of the overlooker, to hasten half-dressed, but not half-fed, to those magazines of British infantile slavery – the worsted mills in the neighbourhood of Bradford!!! (Leeds Mercury, 16 October 1830.)*

In Parliament the movement was led by Sadler until he lost his seat in 1832, following the first Reform Bill. However, the great philanthropist, Lord Ashley, took up the struggle and saw it through to its close in 1850.

In 1833, Lord Ashley introduced a Ten Hours Bill into Parliament. It was not passed, but it did provoke the government into appointing a Royal Commission to investigate the factories. This Commission did their job thoroughly. They went into the most important textile districts where they visited the factories and questioned witnesses at their place of work. They took good care to see and talk to the ordinary people as well as the employers. The Commissioners sent their findings to the Central Board in London, whose chairman was Edwin Chadwick.

The Report found that the large, new mills were well-built, healthy and safe. There was little cruelty in them in the shape of beatings, but what was cruel were the long hours which led to bad health and crooked limbs. The small, old mills, on the other hand, had all the same evils of long hours and were unhealthy and unsafe as well. Moreover there was a certain amount of deliberate cruelty in them. Perhaps most important of all, the Commissioners found that few employers obeyed the law, and they advised Parliament to pass an Act making effective regulations.

This happened in 1833. Parliament followed the advice of the Commission closely – indeed it was Chadwick who drafted the Bill. We call it the Factories Regulation Act or, sometimes, Althorp's Act, as Althorp introduced it to Parliament. It applied to almost all textile mills, and said that in those places:

No child under the age of nine was to be employed.

Children from nine to thirteen should work for no more than forty-eight hours a week and no more than nine hours in one day.

Young people from thirteen to eighteen should work for no more than sixty-nine hours a week, and no more than twelve hours in one day.

Children under thirteen must attend school for at least twelve hours a week.

No child was to be employed, unless he had a certificate of age given by a doctor. (This law was passed at a time when there were no such things as birth certificates.)

But most important of all, there were to be four Inspectors of Factories, assisted by Superintendents, whose work was to ensure that the law was obeyed. It only remained to be seen whether the Factory Inspectors would do better than the magistrates.

There was every chance that they would, because they were to work full-time, they were properly paid, and they were dedicated men. Above all, they were neither factory owners, nor the friends of factory owners. But they did not have an easy task, since few people in the factory districts liked the new Act, whether they were employers, or parents. How effective the Inspectors were was shown by a further report, the *Report of the Royal Commission on Mills and Factories*, in 1841.

This Commission reported many changes for the better. Children no longer did night work and it was unusual for children under nine to work in a factory. But employers were not obeying the law in other ways. Children were often working longer hours than they should and they were not having proper breaks for meals. They could only work for nine hours, but employers were determined to keep their factories going for twelve or more. To do this they employed more children and put them on a complicated system of relays. This was so involved that it was almost impossible for an Inspector to carry out a proper check. Clearly, Parliament would have to pass another Act.

Parliament and child labour

This happened in 1844. The new Act said that no child should work more than six and a half hours a day, and that all these hours must come either in the morning, or in the afternoon. Employers now had to have two quite separate shifts – one group of children who worked in the morning, and another who worked in the afternoon. This meant an end to the complicated relay system and it was now much easier for an Inspector to check the hours that any child worked.

The Act tried to do more about education. A child now had to go to school for three hours a day, and since he was only in the factory for half a day, he could spend part of the other half in an ordinary school during normal school hours.

Young people of thirteen to eighteen were also helped; they could now work no more than twelve hours in any one day and no more than sixty-nine in a week. This rule also applied to women, which was a big step forward, for it was the first time that Parliament had given protection to any adults.

Finally, at the very end of our period, the long battle for the ten hour day came to an end. In 1847 John Fielden persuaded Parliament to pass an Act cutting the hours of young persons and women yet again – this time to ten hours a day, with a maximum of fifty-eight in the week. This Act was found to have several weaknesses, but they were put right, largely by another Act introduced into Parliament in 1850 by Lord Ashley.

Still nothing had been said directly about adult men workers. Cutting the hours of children to six and a half a day had not helped them a lot, because mill-owners had employed one shift of children in the mornings, and another in the afternoons, so that the factories could carry on for thirteen hours. But it was impossible to find a way round the time limits for women and young persons, and the mills could not work without them. In effect, the Ten Hours Act helped everyone.

So ended a struggle that had gone on for fifty years. It is depressing to realise that we have been all the time looking only at cotton and woollen factories. What about other industries? Parliament had done something. In 1845 there was an Act which cut down the hours children could work at calico printing. Even more important was the Mines Act of 1844, which prohibited entirely the employment of women, girls and young boys in coal mines. This was largely the result of Lord Ashley's efforts.

Wool, cotton and coal were three important industries – but many thousands of children worked in other trades. These Acts of Parliament did nothing for the apprentices of the south Staffordshire locksmiths, the pin-makers of Warrington, or farmers' boys all over the country. It was one thing to inspect and control large concerns like factories and mines, but it was almost impossible to visit hundreds of little workshops. The only real cure was to build enough schools and then make all children go to them, which did not happen until well into the second half of the nineteenth century.

ORIGINAL SOURCES

Baines, Edward. *History of the Cotton Manufacture in Great Britain.* 1835.
Ure, A. *The Cotton Manufacture of Great Britain.* 1836.
Ure, A. *Philosophy of Manufacture.* 1835. These three books are all in support of the factory system.
Dodd, William. *The Factory System Illustrated.* 1842.
Fielden, John. *The Curse of the Factory System.* 1836. These two books take the opposing view.
Hodder, E. *Life of Lord Shaftesbury.* 3 vols. 1866.

FURTHER READING

Dunlop, O. J. *English Apprenticeship and Child Labour.* Fisher Unwin, 1912.
Hammond, J. L. and Hammond, Barbara. *Lord Shaftesbury.* Cass, London, 1969.
Ward, J. T. *The Factory Movement 1830–1850.* 1963. A clear account of factory agitation and legislation.

LITERARY SOURCES

Dickens, Charles. *David Copperfield.* Penguin, Harmondsworth, 1969. (Chapter 11: working at Murdstone and Grimby's.)
Dickens, Charles. *Oliver Twist.* Penguin, Harmondsworth, 1970. (Chapters 3 and 4: pauper apprentices.)
Disraeli, Benjamin. *Sybil.* World's Classics Series, O.U.P., Oxford. (Chapter on locksmith's workshop in Willenhall. This follows closely the Appendix to the Second Report of the Children's Employment Commission, 1842.)

6 Poverty

MOST OF THIS BOOK IS ABOUT POVERTY. WE CAN SEE ITS CAUSES IN UNEMPLOYMENT, in the decline of old-established crafts, in disease, in ignorance, and in the immigration of many poor Irish labourers. We can see its results in slum towns, foul living conditions, child labour, crime and social unrest. What we shall see in this chapter is how people coped with the problem.

There was a complicated system of poor relief which dated from the reign of Queen Elizabeth. Parliament made several laws in her reign and, then, in 1601, consolidated them all in one Poor Law Act. The main idea behind this Act was that each parish was to be responsible for its own poor. The occupiers of property were to pay rates and the money was to be spent in a variety of ways. If adults who were fit and well became unemployed, then the parish was to buy materials and give them work. If there were any orphans, then the parish was to educate and apprentice them. If there were people either too old or too sick to look after themselves, then the parish was to give them food, clothing and somewhere to live.

This was not such a kind Act as it sounds for everything was done to humiliate people who came to the parish for help. Ratepayers begrudged the money they had to pay for the relief of the poor and tried to discourage them by making it seem a disgrace to be in want. There were also severe penalties for vagrants, who were unemployed beggars that wandered round from place to place, settling nowhere. These sturdy beggars terrorized the countryside, and in return the authorities whipped and branded them whenever they could catch them.

Parliament passed another important measure in 1662, the Act of Settlement. Some parishes were more generous than others, and so poor people tended to move to the villages where they felt they would be most comfortable. This put up the cost of poor relief in the generous parishes, and their ratepayers objected. The aim of the Act of Settlement was to meet these objections. If someone moved into a parish and it looked as if he might be a charge on the rates, then the overseers of the poor or the churchwardens could apply to the magistrates to have him removed. As long as the application was made within forty days of the arrival of the stranger, he would have to go back where he belonged. This was the parish where he had a settlement and was normally the place where he had been born. It was possible to acquire a settlement in another parish. Anyone who paid rates had a settlement, for the law was only directed against the poor; a woman who married became settled in her husband's parish; serving an apprenticeship in a place gave a right of settlement, as was being hired as a servant for a year or longer.

The Speenhamland system

As it would have been foolish to make a man stay unemployed in his own parish when there was work for him to do elsewhere, the law allowed him to move house for as long as he pleased, subject to the condition that his own parish gave him a certificate to say they would have him back if ever he became a charge on the rates.

Parliament later altered the law in many ways and local authorities did much to change its spirit by the way they administered it, but the Elizabethan Poor Law of 1601 and the Act of Settlement of 1662 remained the foundations of the system of poor relief in this country until the Poor Law Amendment Act of 1834.

We must now see how the system worked at the time of the Industrial Revolution.

As we already know, the parish was the unit responsible for the care of the poor, and it was not fit for such a heavy responsibility. In 1831 in England and Wales there were over 15 500 parishes. They differed enormously in size and wealth, but over 10 000 of them were small, being made up of 200 families or less. It is not surprising that the treatment of the poor varied a lot, and that most parishes were unable to cope properly.

To administer each parish there was a body called the vestry. It had this name because its meeting place was sometimes the vestry of the church. In most parishes all the ratepayers had the right to attend the vestry meeting, although in practice, the only ones to turn up were those who thought they had something to gain or lose.

One important duty of the vestry was to appoint the parish officers, such as the churchwardens, the constable, the headboroughs, and the men who concern us here, the overseers of the poor. The work of the overseers was to decide how much money would be needed for poor relief, assess the ratepayers of the parish, and collect the rates from them. Each week they had to meet the paupers who came to claim their relief, decide how good each one's claim was and pay him accordingly.

The overseers were appointed for a year, although sometimes the vestry would choose several so that each need serve only for a part of the year. By the time they had learnt a little about their work and had found out who had genuine need for help and who had not, it was time for them to retire.

There was no one way of giving relief to the poor. No two parishes would have exactly the same system, but, broadly speaking, there were four methods. These were the Speenhamland or allowance system, the roundsman system, the labour rate, and the workhouse.

The Speenhamland system is the best known, and was the most common. It started during the Napoleonic wars when prices rose so quickly that many labouring families were in distress. To help the poor in their own part of the country, the Berkshire magistrates decided to meet and fix a minimum wage that all employers would have to pay. This meeting took place at Speen, near Newbury, in 1795. But the Berkshire magistrates changed their minds, for they left wages alone and instead fixed a system of allowances. These allowances were tied to the price of bread, which was the main item in the labourers' diet, and which they used to buy by the gallon – a gallon loaf weighing eight pounds eleven ounces. When the price of this was 1s, each labourer was to have 3s for himself, and 1s 6d for each of his family. If the man's wages did not come up to this amount, then the overseers were to make up the difference out of the rates. If the price of bread went up, the allowance would too, so that whatever happened to prices, no one need go short. This was

The allowance system

called the Speenhamland system because it originated at Speen. Magistrates in other counties thought it a good idea and it spread widely, especially in the agricultural counties of the south of England. On the face of it, it was a good and kind plan but unfortunately, there were results which the Berkshire magistrates did not foresee.

In the first place so many labourers applied for help that the rates jumped up by leaps and bounds. In 1775 the country spent £1½ million on poor relief; by 1803 it was over £4 million, and by 1818 it was £8 million. The burden was not spread evenly either, for some parts of the country were more badly hit than others. There were villages where landlords had to reduce the rents of their farms to five shillings an acre, or one-fifth of the national average, because the poor rates were so heavy. At Cholesbury, in Buckinghamshire, the poor rates were so high that the tenants just left their farms, and the tradesmen their businesses.

Next, labourers as a class became thoroughly demoralised. At one time it had been thought a disgrace to go to the parish for help, but wages were so low and prices were so high that they had no choice. They soon found that it was easier to apply for poor relief than it was to work hard. The money they drew depended, not on how hard they worked, but on the price of bread and the size of their families. The man who worked hard for his master was likely to be mocked by the other villagers, and reliable, industrious workmen were sometimes hard to find.

Another bad result was that some landowners set out deliberately to depopulate their villages. This could only happen where a parish belonged to one man, or to a few determined men who were willing to work together. If a house fell vacant they pulled it down, and however much the population went up they would refuse to build new houses. Places like this were known as closed parishes. Inevitably, many of the inhabitants had to go and live in open parishes or in towns, where the land and property were divided among so many owners that there could be no conspiracy of this kind against the poor. Keeping the population down meant that there were fewer people who might become a charge on the rates. There was no danger of a labour shortage for in the adjoining parishes there would be a surplus of workmen that they could call on during the busy seasons of the year and send packing when they were not wanted. The losers were the ratepayers in the open parishes, and the labourers who had to walk long distances to work. We can see the results of this policy on two Norfolk villages:

	1821		1841	
	Houses	Population	Houses	Population
Lakenham	403	1875	973	4006
Caistor	38	164	35	147

Lakenham was, of course, an open village, while Caistor was closed.

If the Speenhamland system had such bad results, why did it go on? In the first place, there was a certain class of tenant farmer who saved money. High rates were something of a nuisance, but he could use them as a reason for paying less rent. What was really important, however, was that the tenant farmers had an excuse to lower wages. They could offer their men much less than they were able to live on, and then tell them to go to the parish for the rest. This was most unfair to the smaller farmers and tradesmen who employed no labour. They had to pay rates in order to save richer men than themselves the expense of giving their workers a decent living wage.

Secondly, the allowance system allowed a good deal of jobbery. It was not hard for a dishonest overseer to embezzle the rates, for there was no one to keep a check on him. It was even easier for an overseer to help his favourites in the parish. If he was a landlord he would help his tenants, so that he was sure of his rent, and if he was a shopkeeper he would help his customers, so that they would pay his bills.

Fear, too, played an important part. Paupers would fire the ricks and smash the machinery of an unpopular overseer, but it was a wider and deeper problem than just that. The early nineteenth century brought social unrest in both town and countryside, while the French Revolution was still very much alive in people's minds. They thought it quite possible that the same could happen in this country, and indeed the farm labourers of the south of England did rise in revolt in 1830. It seemed that the working classes must be kept contented whatever the cost, and since employers would not pay good wages the ratepayers had to foot the bill.

Another method of giving poor relief was the roundsman system. Under this, the able-bodied paupers went the rounds of the various employers, who took them on at a low wage which might be fixed at an auction. At the Northamptonshire village of Sulgrave the old men were put up for hire each week, and fetched anything between 1s 6d and 3s, according to the season of the year. This was nothing like enough for them to live on, so when they had finished their week's work the employer signed a ticket which they took to the overseer, who made up their wages to something more reasonable. This was not unlike the allowance system, the difference being that it was meant to help the unemployed, and not people who were working for wages too low to live on.

Yet another system was the labour rate. Under this, each ratepayer had to employ a number of paupers, and pay them full wages without any allowance from the parish. At first sight this seems a better system, but in practice it was most unfair. The problem was how to assess the labour rate. It could be based on the acreage of a farm, but then a man with an arable farm would benefit because he needed men to work his fields. On the other hand, a man with much grassland would find he had to employ men for whom he had no work. Perhaps a man would be told to take workers according to the amount of rates he owed in money, but again this was unfair. Wealthy men, with large farms or businesses could use the extra help; but a man working a small farm or business with the help of his own family found he was employing men he did not need. The labour rate was a wasteful and clumsy system; nothing shows this more clearly than the habit of letting machines stand idle and sending unemployed paupers to thresh corn with the flail, just to keep them busy through the winter.

The allowance system, the roundsman system and the labour rate were all forms of outdoor relief. But in some parishes there was indoor relief as well. This meant that the pauper left his own home and came to live in a workhouse.

One of the earliest workhouses was started in Bristol in 1695 by John Cary. His idea was that the paupers should be brought under supervision and made to earn their keep. An Act of 1723 gave this idea legal blessing. Any parish could, if it

Workhouses

wished, open a workhouse and set its paupers to work. But paupers were unreliable and most of them were unskilled, so it was usually impossible to make a profit from them. By the end of the eighteenth century Parliament recognised this and in 1782 passed an Act, known as Gilbert's Act. This law allowed parishes to combine to set up workhouses, if they wished, but they were to be for the 'impotent poor' – those who were too young, too old, or too sick to live on their own. Able-bodied paupers were not to live in the workhouse, but were to have outdoor relief. According to the 1723 Act the workhouse was to be a place of hard labour; according to Gilbert's Act, it was to be a place of refuge.

As there was no government supervision, workhouses varied a great deal. A purpose-built house, in a wealthy parish, and under a good master, might well be a fit place to live in, but this is what many were like:

> *In parishes overburthened with poor we usually find the building called a workhouse occupied by 60 or 80 children (under the care, perhaps, of a pauper), about 20 or 30 able-bodied paupers of both sexes, and probably an equal number of aged and impotent persons, the proper objects of relief. Amidst these, the mothers of bastard children and prostitutes live without shame and associate freely with the youth, who have also the examples and conversation of the frequent inmates of the county gaol, the poacher, the vagrant, the decayed beggar, and other characters of the worst description. To these may often be added a solitary blind person, one or two idiots and not unfrequently are heard among the rest, the incessant ravings of some neglected lunatic. In such receptacles the sick poor are often immured. (Report from the Commissioners Inquiring into the Administration and Practical Operation of the Poor Laws. 1834, p. 303.)*

Such was the state of affairs in the first part of the nineteenth century, but by the early 1830s times were changing. The political turmoils of the Reform Bill days passed by; the middle classes won the vote and a voice in the government, so they were contented. Moreover, trade was booming, wages were rising, unemployment falling, and food prices were low, so the working classes, too, were tolerably happy. The new Whig government felt strong enough to tackle the thorny problem of poor relief and in 1832 appointed a Royal Commission to look into it.

There was to be a central Board of Commissioners which included two bishops, an economist with the curious name of Nassau Senior and a man called Thomas Frankland Lewis, of whom we shall hear more. The Assistant Commissioner who reported on East and North London was Edwin Chadwick, and in the end it was Chadwick who did more towards writing the final report than all of the full Commissioners put together.

As a young man, Chadwick had come under the influence of the philosopher, Jeremy Bentham. Bentham employed Chadwick as his secretary, and in spite of a great difference in their ages, the two became firm friends. It was Chadwick who nursed Bentham during the illness which finally killed him.

Bentham was a utilitarian. There were – and still are – people who believe we should respect traditions, and that institutions which are well-established should not be changed lightly; Bentham was just the opposite. Put simply, his test of anything was to ask whether it was of use. If it was, then it might remain; if it was not,

BILL of FARE.

	Breakfast.	Dinner.	Supper.
Sunday	Bread and Butter, and Half a Pint of Beer.	Seven Ounces of Meat, Vegetables and a Pint of Beer.	Bread and Cheese, and Butter, and a Pint of Beer.
Monday	Broth, or Bread and Butter.	Milk Pottage.	Bread and Butter, and a Pint of Beer.
Tuesday	Water Gruel.	Seven Ounces of boiled Meat, and a Pint of Beer.	Bread and Cheese, and a Pint of Beer.
Wednesday	Broth.	Milk Pottage.	Bread and Butter, and a Pint of Beer.
Thursday	Water Gruel.	Seven Ounces of boiled Meat, and a Pint of Beer.	Bread and Cheese, and a Pint of Beer.
Friday	Broth.	Rice Milk.	Bread and Butter, and a Pint of Beer.
Saturday	Water Gruel.	Legs of Beef, and a Pint of Beer.	Bread and Cheese, and a Pint of Beer.

N. B. Each Person to be allowed 14 Ounces of Bread *per* Day, but on Banyan Days 12 Ounces each.—Allowance of Cheese 2 oz. and Butter to be 1 oz.

From the First of *November* to the First of *April* Half a Bushel of Coals *per* Day.—From the First of *November* to the Tenth of *February* One Candle in the Dinner-Room each Night, except *Sunday*, then Two to be allowed; from the Tenth of *February* to the Tenth of *March*, One in Two Nights; from the Tenth of *March* to the Tenth of *September* no Candles, and from the Tenth of *September* to the First of *November* One Candle in Two Nights.

Bill of Fare. This is the food given in a house for old people. It was not a workhouse in that it was owned privately and the inmates had to pay rent. The food in a workhouse proper would have been a good deal less attractive than this Courtesy of Guildhall Library, City of London.

then it should go. Everything must be orderly, streamlined and efficient. But how was this to come about? Bentham put forward an idea which is commonplace to us, but which was new in his day. Where there is any need for reform the state must step in and see that it is carried out. Bentham greatly admired what had happened in France under Napoleon. The privileges of the nobility, the church, the guilds and the towns were all swept away. The old provincial administration went too, and France was divided into departments, equal in size, and under the close control of a powerful central government.

Chadwick learnt all this from Bentham, and was eager to use his new ideas. It is not difficult to imagine what he thought of the administration of the poor laws. He found chaos where there should have been order, he found extravagance where there should have been economy, and he found complete local independence where, he thought, there should have been strong central control. His arguments were so convincing that he was made a full Commissioner. He then persuaded Nassau Senior to accept his views, and virtually wrote the report of the Commission himself. It was published in 1834.

What attracted Chadwick were the parishes that had been depauperized. In these places one or two determined men had taken charge: they had stopped giving relief to everyone and helped only those who were in genuine need. One of these was Southwell, where George Nicholls was responsible for the depauperization. Nicholls had two golden rules: in the first place no one had any relief unless he or she came to live in the workhouse, and secondly, the workhouse was made so unattractive that no one would want to live in it unless he was desperate. The keeper had to treat and feed the paupers properly, but there were other regulations as well:

Men and women, even husbands and wives, had to live apart.
No one could go out except to leave the workhouse for good.
No one could have visitors.
There was to be no tobacco or beer
All able-bodied paupers were to work.

It was probably this last rule that was the most effective in driving away people who wanted relief. Attached to the workhouse there was a yard and in it a pile of old bones and the work consisted of smashing these with a sledge hammer. This is what happened:

> The workhouse keeper only had occasion to try two men with the bone plan. One said immediately, with sulky violence, that he would never break bones for the parish when he could go out and get something for breaking stones for others, and he went out the next day. The other said it hurt his back to bend so much, and he would leave the next day, which he did. The third had a hole to dig, which he liked so little that he went off on the third day. He had been, for nine or ten years before, one of the most troublesome men in the parish, but he went off very quietly, saying that he did not complain of the victuals or accommodation, but if he was to work, would work for himself; he has never troubled the parish since, and now he gets his own living in a brick yard, and by thrashing and other jobs, and has done so ever since. (Ibid., p. 248.)

This was in a parish where paupers had come in large numbers to claim relief, or rather demand it, for they had regularly threatened the overseer who had had to take about a dozen to court each week. Now they were told that they could not have money to take away and spend as they liked. If they needed relief they could have it, but only by coming to live in the workhouse and obeying its rules. Almost at once, nearly all of them decided to do without the help of the parish and find work for themselves.

Refuge for the destitute.
This was maintained by charity. People who would otherwise have slept in the streets at least had a roof over their heads, and straw on which to lie.
Courtesy of Mansell Collection.

This seemed to Chadwick to be the solution for the whole country. The big mistake, he thought, was to give outdoor relief to the able-bodied, and that should stop. There might be people who were starving and in genuine need, and no one wanted them to die. To separate these people from the frauds there was to be the workhouse test. Was the applicant willing to live in the workhouse, or not? If he was, obviously he was in need, and he would be admitted to receive food, clothing and shelter. If he was not willing to live in the workhouse, then obviously he was not in need, and he could go away empty handed. The system was as simple, as logical, and as efficient as Bentham himself could have wished.

There was the danger that workhouse life might be more attractive than life outside, and to guard against this Chadwick stated the principle of 'less eligibility'. The life of the pauper must be 'less eligible', that is less attractive, than that of the poorest independent labourer. As soon as people realised that they would be

57

Poor Law Amendment Act

better off 'on the parish' than working for a living, they gave up trying and flocked to the overseer for poor relief. To stop this workhouses had to be places where life was dull and unpleasant. They had to be well regulated, and there should be no cruelty in them, but they had to be places where no one would live if he had the choice. The Southwell rules seemed admirable to Chadwick.

Along with the workhouse test and 'less eligibility' there was to be strong central control. Chadwick advised a central board with considerable power to compel obedience from the local authorities.

Local administration, too, needed reform. Most parishes were too small to set up efficient workhouses, so they were to combine into Unions. In each Union there was to be a Board of Guardians elected by the ratepayers, and this had to appoint paid officials, such as the workhouse master and the overseer. There were to be no more amateurs mishandling the ratepayers' money and encouraging idleness among the poor.

The Poor Law Commissioners' Report was, thanks to Chadwick, a forceful and well-argued document. Parliament accepted most of its ideas and passed the Poor Law Amendment Act of 1834 to enforce them. To sum up, these were the main provisions of the Act:

Parishes were to combine to form unions.

Each union was to be governed by a Board of Guardians, elected by the ratepayers. The Guardians were to appoint salaried officials – overseer, workhouse master, medical officers – to look after the poor.

There was to be a central board of three Poor Law Commissioners, helped by twelve Assistant Commissioners, whose duty it was to keep an eye on the Guardians and see they did their work properly.

The next step was for the Government to choose the three Commissioners to make up the central board. They appointed a man called Shaw-Lefevre, because he had powerful friends in the Whig Government, but they then had to please the Tories, so they chose Thomas Frankland Lewis, who had been a member of the 1832 Commission. The third member was George Nicholls, the man who had depauperized Southwell. Chadwick, who had done most of the work, was passed over, much to his disgust, though he was given the post of Secretary to the Board and told that he would have a say in guiding its policy.

It was now the duty of the Board to enforce the Poor Law Amendment Act, but almost at once it ran into trouble. Unfortunately, Parliament had differed from the report in one important respect, and this was over the powers of the Board. When it started work the Board found it was unable to compel Boards of Guardians to do all that it wanted. It could stop them doing what it disliked – for example, giving outdoor relief – but it could not require positive, useful work, like the building of good workhouses and schools. Moreover, the Poor Law Office was not a happy place. Chadwick was full of enthusiasm for his work, but like many dedicated men he was too sure he was right, and unwilling to listen to reason. He had no sense of humour and was often ill-mannered. Unfortunately one of the Commissioners, Thomas Frankland Lewis, was even more difficult, because of his disdainful attitude to the world in general. He and Chadwick took an instant dislike to one another and were soon bitter enemies.

Nor was there just a clash of personalities; there was one of policy as well. Chadwick wanted to encourage the revival of agriculture, the spread of education, and the building and staffing of decent workhouses. In other words, he wanted to remove some of the causes of poverty. The members of the Board thought otherwise – they felt that their duty was simply to stop people applying for poor relief. It did not matter how the poor suffered, as long as they did not become a charge on the rates. Since he was only the Secretary to the Board, Chadwick could not compel its members to accept his ideas, and as they thoroughly disliked him, he had no chance of winning them over by persuasion.

The Board now set out to depauperize England, as George Nicholls had depauperized Southwell. They made some progress, so that by 1838 nearly all the parishes in the south of England were grouped into unions. Poor rates decreased from £7 million in 1832 to £4 million in 1837. It took longer to provide well regulated workhouses, but gradually they began to appear. In a few of them life was intolerable, for example at Andover. Here the paupers were so starved that they fought over the scraps of rotting meat that clung to the bones they had to crush. Andover was exceptional, but no workhouse was a pleasant place to live – the Guardians of the unions took good care of that. Most of them drew up rules very like the ones George Nicholls had made for Southwell, and these were quite enough to ensure a drab and miserable existence without resorting to cruelty or starvation diets. The poor developed a dread of the workhouse and would only come to it if they absolutely had to – just, indeed, as Chadwick had planned. Here, however, the success of the Board stopped.

The poor Law Board had concentrated mainly on one problem, which was the able-bodied labourer who preferred to live on the parish rather than look for work. To this problem it saw but one solution – offer such a man the workhouse, or nothing. But laziness was only one thing among many that caused pauperism. There were other forces much more powerful, for example, a trade depression, bringing mass unemployment in the industrial towns. By 1837 the years of prosperity were over, and in 1841 the country was in the grip of one of the worst depressions in its history. It was just at this time that the Poor Law Commissioners tried to enforce the new Poor Law in the north of England.

Here Chadwick's principles just did not apply. In the first place, there had been no allowance system of any significance. Secondly, when a man was unemployed it was not because he was too lazy to find work, but because there was no work to be had. It was futile to use the workhouse to frighten a man into finding a job if there was no job for him to find. It was small wonder that the people were in an ugly mood. Through no fault of their own they were thrown out of work, and the only way to avoid starvation was to submit to imprisonment in the workhouse. There were riots and disorder, with mobs attacking workhouses and poor law officials. The Board had no choice but to allow outdoor relief.

In the south of England, the Board's policy met with more success, and we have already seen how the allowance system came to an end. But little more was achieved. When James Caird wrote his letters on farming in England in 1850, he found many of the evils mentioned in the Poor Law Report of 1834. Wages were still low, even though the allowance system had gone; in one Wiltshire parish, the

Surplus labourers

farmers were paying their men only 6s a week. The reason was that there were too many labourers for too few jobs. Moreover, nothing had been done to stop the labour rate, and employers were having to take men and give them work, whether they needed the help or not. Caird found that there were still farmers who had threshing machines, setting labourers to thresh barley with flails, just to give them something to do through the winter. Again, this was due to a surplus of labourers.

Yet another evil that remained was that of open and closed parishes, so that some men were living four miles, or more, from their work. This was in the days before public transport, so they had to tramp for well over an hour each morning and evening.

The problems of the surplus labourers in some areas, and of the open and closed parishes were both due to the law of settlement which the Act of 1834 had not touched. Families felt tied to the places where they had a settlement, and where they could have poor relief, if they needed it. Elsewhere there might be a shortage of workers and they could easily have found jobs; but they would have lost their security, so they preferred to stay where they were.

The tragedy lay in this, that the Poor Law Board lacked the power and the will to help the poor to lead happier and more prosperous lives. It did a great deal in the south to stop people applying for poor relief unless they desperately needed it, but this was only a fraction of the problem. Possibly only one fifth of all paupers were able-bodied males, and most of these would have been in genuine need. While the board did enough — and perhaps more than enough — to cure pauperism, it did next to nothing to cure poverty.

ORIGINAL SOURCES

Administration of the Poor Law in the Andover Union. Parliamentary Papers 1846 Vol. V.
Baxter, W. *The Book of the Bastilles*. 1841. These two are both adverse accounts of the operation of the 1834 Act.
Eden, F. M. *State of the Poor*. 1797. A comprehensive account of the problem of poverty.
Report from the Commissioners Inquiring into the Administration and Practical Operation of the Poor Laws. Parliamentary Papers 1834 Vols XXVII and XXIX.

FURTHER READING

Anstruther, I. *The Scandal of the Andover Workhouse*. Bles, London, 1973. A description of the Poor Law and its abuses.
Finer, S. E. *The Life and Times of Sir Edwin Chadwick*. Methuen, London, 1970.
Rose, W. E. *The Relief of Poverty 1834–1914*. Studies in Economic History, Macmillan, Basingstoke. Excellent short account of the working of the Poor Law.
Watson, Roger. *Edwin Chadwick, Poor Law and Public Health*. Then and There Series, Longman, London, 1969. A short book, but very vivid and clear in its descriptions.

LITERARY SOURCES

Dickens, Charles. *Little Dorrit*. Penguin, Harmondsworth, 1967. (Chapter 31: pauper allowed out to visit his family.)

Dickens, Charles. *Oliver Twist*. Penguin, Harmondsworth, 1970. (Chapters 1 and 2: workhouse life.)

Dickens, Charles. *Our Mutual Friend*. Penguin, Harmondsworth, 1971. (Book I, Chapter 16 and Book II, Chapter 8: Betty Higden's horror of the workhouse and of poor relief.)

Dickens, Charles. *Reprinted Pieces*. Everyman's Library, Dent, London, 1970. A Walk in the Workhouse.

Dickens, Charles. *Sketches by Boz*. Everyman's Library, Dent, London, 1968. (Our Parish, chapter 1: parish officers and giving poor relief.)

Dickens, Charles. *The Uncommercial Traveller*. Everyman's Library, Dent, London, 1969. (Chapter 3: Wapping workhouse; chapter 29: almshouse.)

7 Domestic habits

IN CHAPTER TWO WE SAW WHAT TOWNS AND HOUSES WERE LIKE. WHAT WE NOW HAVE to do is to look at the lives which people led in them.

Care of the home

The houses were poor enough to start with, but the people made them intolerable. There were several reasons for this: in the first place, most women went to work, as well as their husbands and children. The whole family came home to find their house cold and dirty and with no meal ready. They were all exhausted by their long hours of work and had no energy for cooking or cleaning. Secondly, few women knew much about housekeeping. Most of them had been at work since they were little girls, and they had never learnt how to look after a home. When a girl married she might not even know how to cook potatoes. Thirdly, the wretched houses would have discouraged all but the most determined woman.

This is a description of what happened to one girl, who had been a servant:

Working class homes. One room has to serve for living, cooking, eating, washing and sleeping
Courtesy of Guildhall Library, City of Library, City of London

A WORKMAN'S HOME
ROSE & CROWN COURT ISLINGTON

SUNDAY MORNING
WORKMANS HOME
LEATHER LANE

Overcrowding
proved to be one
of the most
intractable social
problems, as,
indeed, it still is
Courtesy of Guildhall
Library,
City of London

Her attention to personal neatness, was very great: her face seemed always as if it were just washed, and with her bright hair neatly combed underneath her snow-white cap, a smooth white apron and her gown and handkerchief, she looked very comely. After a year or two she married a serving man who was obliged to take a house as near his place of work as possible. The cottages in the neighbourhood were of the most wretched kind, mere hovels, built of rough stones and covered with ragged thatch. After they had been married about two years, I visited the home of the servant I have been describing. But what a change had come over her! Her face was dirty, and her tangled hair hung over her eyes. Her cap was ill-washed and slovenly put on. Her whole dress was very untidy, and looked dirty and slatternly: every-thing about her seemed wretched and neglected (except her little child) and she seemed very discontented. She seemed aware of the change that there must be in her appearance since I had last seen her, for she immediately began to complain of her house. The wet came in at the door of the only room, and when it rained, through every part of the roof also: large drops fell on her as she lay in her bed: in short she had found it impossible to keep things in order, so she had gradually ceased to make any exertions. Her condition had been borne down by the conditions of the house. Then her husband was dissatisfied with his home and with her. (Chadwick, op. cit., p. 195.)

In later years someone asked Lord Shaftesbury, 'Does the sty make the pig, or does the pig make the sty?' He said he had no doubt that if the poor had better houses they would lead more decent lives.

Food and clothing

Furniture was inadequate. There might be a simple deal table, with some hard chairs, or planks on bricks for seats. There might be a bed, or there might just be a heap of sacking and straw on the floor. Probably there would be no chest of drawers, so the clothes would be put in boxes instead. For crockery, there would be an assortment of odd cups, saucers and bowls, with a few cheap knives, forks and spoons. Food was cooked in kettles or pans on the living-room fire.

The diet of the poorest workers was mainly bread and potatoes. The potatoes were for their midday meal and to go with them there might be suet, or bacon or herrings, but few families had fresh meat regularly. For breakfast, tea and supper they had weak tea and bread, sometimes spread with lard. It was no trouble to prepare a meal of bread and tea, and it was cheap. In the north they often had porridge made with milk, but milk was not used a lot outside the dairying counties.

Much of the food was bad, especially the fish and meat. A visitor to the Wolverhampton market said there was no need to go up to a fish stall to see the quality of the wares – you could tell from twenty feet away. The meat was as bad. The butchers smeared fresh blood over stale joints, and powdered the fat white. Their worst meat stayed outside the markets in carts until it was dark, and then they sold it by candle light. Much of the meat came from animals that had died of old age or disease, and from calves born prematurely. This veal hung in strips that flapped about in the breeze. It was sold by length, not weight. 'It isn't bad,' the butcher would explain, 'only a little young.'

Clearly a diet like this was low in food value. It is small wonder that children grew up deformed – if they grew up at all.

The exceptions were the miners, who fed themselves well whenever they had the chance. One man said of the colliers of Staffordshire:

> They always live upon the best of everything. They keep all feast-days religiously, from Shrove-tide pancakes to the Michaelmas goose. It is notorious that on the first day of 'Ducks and green peas', the colliers buy up all that there are in the market. (Parliamentary Papers, 1842, Vol. XV, q. 30.)

Most families managed to have a good meal at Christmas – but they had to ask their baker to cook it for them, as few homes were equipped with their own ovens.

Clothing was poor. Poorer families patched their clothes again and again and did not buy new ones until the old ones were falling to pieces. Boys and men wore trousers, a jacket, a waistcoat, a shirt, and wooden-soled shoes. They would have no underwear and probably no socks. Girls and women wore long dresses and pinafores. They would have no change of clothing, so they washed their shirts or dresses at the week-end and hoped they would dry over night. They wore the same clothes winter and summer – the only difference was that boys left their jackets off when it was hot.

Fortunately, most clothing was now of cotton, which people could wash easily and dry quickly. It is not as warm as wool but it is easier to keep clean and free from vermin – though there were, indeed, too many who did not bother at all about dirt and lice.

Again, it was the colliers who had the best. They had Sunday suits and could show off a bit. One witness describes them, clothed in black, with white neck-cloths that made them look a bit like parsons. He thought this sober dress was due to the influence of the Methodists.

We have seen in the chapter on the state of the towns that poor people found it hard to keep clean. As there were no drains there was bound to be filth all round the houses; with as many as fifty people sharing each privy, these places were only too often unfit for use. A clergyman who started a school for the poor at Dowlais, in South Wales, discovered that the children did not know how to use the school privies – the teacher had to show them.

Shortage of water made washing a problem. When a woman washed clothes, she would not throw the water away, but would keep it and use it for one lot of clothes after another.

Children sometimes stayed dirty. Their mothers might wash their faces and hands now and again, and a good mother would strip and wash her child once a week, but some parents hardly washed their children at all, and this was a habit they kept through life. A police inspector who knew the poorer parts of Edinburgh often asked people when they last washed. Quite commonly the answer was, 'When I was last in prison.'

We can see what dirt and neglect meant in a home from this description of a house in Bath:

> *The room was in a horrible state, and there were excrements all over the place: in fact the place was reeking with the smell of filth. The two beds were black and shining with body grease, but there was no covering on them. Such bedding as there was, was stinking and rotten and covered with filth, while on the bed was lying a little boy, naked except for a piece of cloth around its neck, thin and emaciated, evidently ill and apparently struggling for breath. The child was sucking from a filthy feeding bottle which contained sour milk curds, while the teat was stinking. I swept maggots from under the bed with a broom, while with the handle of the broom I stirred up maggots from the bed itself. (Bath Chronicle, 17 June 1852.)*

In this house there was neglect as well as the problems of shortage of water and sanitation. Provided they could get water, most people kept clean. One Lancashire manufacturer had water piped into the houses of his work-people and he said that they and their homes were much cleaner as a result. A visitor to a mining village in Durham found he had to be careful walking past the cottages just after the miners finished work.

> *Upon their entrance into their little cottages they proceed to strip and wash themselves. Thus, as to time, the hour of retirement with artisans and mechanics in towns and cities, is to colliers the hour of washing. It is as well to know this, when you are passing the pit villages at this time, if you have any dislike to soap suds, which are now repeatedly ejected from the doors. (J. R. Leifchild, Our Coal Fields and Coal Pits, p. 193.)*

In 1842 a visitor to Willenhall found it miserable and poor. However, it had one

Ventilation

thing in its favour – there was no shortage of water, since almost every court and alley had its own pump. He wrote:

> Amidst all the squalor of bare and dilapidated abodes and general destitution, it very frequently happens that the inside of the poorest house is perfectly clean.
>
> I have entered the houses and hovels of journeymen locksmiths and key-makers, indiscriminately and unexpectedly, and seen the utmost destitution: no furniture in the room below, but a broken board for a table and a piece of plank laid across bricks for a seat: with the wife hungry – almost crying with hunger and in rags: yet the floor was perfectly clean. I have gone upstairs and seen a bed where a husband, his wife and three children slept, and with no other article in the room of any kind whatever, except the bed. Yet the clothes on the bed were perfectly clean: so was the floor: so were the stairs: they were not merely clean, they were really white, and more resembled the boards in the dairy of a large farm-house than anything that could have been anticipated of the wretched hovel of a poor locksmith of Willenhall. (Parliamentary Papers, 1842, Vol. XV, q. 40.)

People who are short of food and clothing feel the cold and this made them afraid of fresh air. In his evidence to the Health of the Towns Commission of 1842, John Brooks, a stocking weaver from Hinckley, explained how he felt. He worked at home, in a small room, for up to sixteen hours a day without opening his window:

> 'Would you rather have bad air which is warmed, than good air that is cold?' 'Yes, I generally prefer the warmth.'
>
> 'Do you consider that that is the general feeling?' 'Yes. I do not know how it is but when we become accustomed to vitiated air, we do not perceive it: it is only annoying in the morning, when we leave another air and come into it, and observe the contrast with the good air. When I have mentioned the injurious effect that this vitiated air had upon my constitution, that I felt it was exhausting my strength, it was looked on as a sort of nonsense and a new fangled notion that was not worth attending to.' (Report of the Commissioners for Inquiring into the State of the Large Towns and Populous Districts, 1844, p. 184.)

Brooks had consumption for which he blamed the bad air. This, of course, was impossible, but we do know that his mother, who lived with him, had the disease, and Brooks had probably caught it from her the more easily because of the lack of ventilation.

Dr Neil Arnott proved there was a close connection between good ventilation and good health. He came across a charity school of some seven hundred children, in which many of the children fell ill from time to time, and sometimes died. The local people turned on the headmaster because they said he was starving the children. But he was feeding them quite well: all the school needed was fresh air. When this was explained to him, he had the school ventilated, and the health of the children improved at once. But most poor people had a dread of the cold and of draughts in their houses. They kept their windows firmly closed, and if anyone broke the glass, they carefully stuffed the hole with old rags.

A vision of the repeal of the window tax.
The repeal of the window tax meant that light and air could get to rooms that had been without.
Reproduced by permission of *Punch*.

We come now to one of the most intractable problems, and one which is still with us in some parts of our large cities – that of overcrowding.

In the poorer parts of Hinckley in the 1840s, families of eight or nine people lived in two rooms – a living room and a bedroom. This seems to have been about average for the country, but there were others who were much worse off. Lord Shaftesbury said that it was quite common for a family to have only one room to itself. Once, he said, he actually found four families sharing a room – one in each corner. They took it in turn to have the place by the fire.

A very bad result, as Lord Shaftesbury said, was that the one room system led to the one bed system. Time and again men like Shaftesbury found a mixture of people of all ages and both sexes living in the same room, and sleeping in the same bed. We have this account from Chadwick's *Sanitary Report* of 1842:

> In Hull I met with a mother about fifty years of age and her son, I should think twenty-five, sleeping in the same bed, and a lodger in the same room. In a cellar in Liverpool, I found a mother and her grown-up daughters sleeping on a bed of chaff on the ground in one corner of the cellar, and in the other corner, three sailors had their bed. I have met with upwards of forty persons sleeping in the same room, married and single, including, of course, children and several young adult persons of either sex. (Chadwick, op. cit., p. 192.)

67

Death

The worst was when animals were brought into the house. A doctor in Tranent in Scotland went to visit some patients and he found ten people living in one small house. There were hens perched up in the rafters and a horse standing tethered to the back of the bed.

A most unpleasant problem that came from overcrowding, was what to do when someone died. One of the most grisly documents we have is Chadwick's report on burials, which was the supplement to his *Sanitary Report*. Many of the details given in the report are better left there and forgotten; this extract is one of the less revolting ones, but it tells us quite as much as we need to know. John Liddle, the Medical Officer of the Whitechapel Union, is giving his evidence:

> *'On the occurrence of a death amongst the labourers, what do you find to be the general condition of the family in relation to the remains? How is the corpse dealt with?'*
>
> *'Nearly the whole of the labouring population have only one room. The corpse is therefore kept in that room where the inmates sleep and have their meals. Sometimes the corpse is stretched on the bed, and the bed clothes are taken off, and the wife and family lie on the floor. Sometimes a board is got, on which the corpse is stretched, and that is sustained on tressles or on chairs. When children die they are frequently laid out on the table.'*
>
> *'What is the usual length of time the corpse is kept?'*
>
> *'The time varies according to the day of the death. Sunday is the day usually chosen for the day of the burial. But if a man die on the Wednesday, the burial will not take place till the Sunday of the week following. Bodies are almost always kept for a full week, frequently longer.'*
>
> *'Do you observe any peculiarity of habit amongst the lower classes accompanying the familiarity with the remains of the dead?'*
>
> *'What I observe when I first visit the room is a degree of indifference to the presence of the corpse; the family is found eating or drinking or pursuing their usual callings, and the children playing. Amongst the middle classes, where there is an opportunity of putting the corpse by itself, there are greater marks of respect and decency.'* (Parliamentary Papers, 1843, Vol. XII, p. 34.)

Wages were very low for many working people, but few of them spent what little they had at all wisely. If a man had a run of good luck and plenty of work to do, then he would live well, but he would not think of putting any money to one side so that he had some savings to tide him over the bad time, which he knew would come sooner or later. The miners of Durham were paid each fortnight, and they had the best of everything during the first few days. During the baff week, as they called the second week after pay day, they lived on little more than tea or coffee.

Women were not wise in their choice of shops. In those days there was a type of grocer called a huckster. This was a man who would sell a single rasher of bacon, an ounce of cheese or a cup of sugar. Of course, none of these little items cost much on their own, but the huckster took a large profit. The housewife who went ten times to the huckster to buy ten rashers of bacon paid far more than her neighbour who went to a grocer and bought all ten at once.

If times were prosperous, working people sometimes wasted food. A visitor to Tyneside said he had often seen a huge girdle cake leaning against the wall of a living room, and the miner's urchins tearing at it with their grubby hands. Sometimes a woman would rip open a packet of sugar, and whenever they felt like having some the children would dip into the bag with a spoon. A Wolverhampton merchant said that the poor of his town thought it too much trouble to cut their bread into neat slices. Instead, they hacked it into all sorts of shapes, and lumps of it were flung on the floor or out into the street. It was a different matter, of course, when times were hard. Hungry people then treasured every crumb.

In his *Sanitary Report* of 1842 Chadwick was at pains to show that it was not just low wages that made people lead miserable lives. He contrasted the state of some families in Manchester:

> *Cellar in York St., a man, his wife, family altogether comprising seven persons: income £2 7s 0d, or 6s 8½d per head; rent 2s. Here the family occupy two filthy damp unwholesome cellars.*

> *In a dwelling house, Store St., one sitting room, one kitchen and two bedrooms, rent 4s per week, a poor widow, with a daughter also a widow, with ten children making together thirteen in family; income £1 6s 0d per week, averaging 2s per head. Here there is every appearance of cleanliness and comfort.*

> *John Scott of Carr Bank, labourer. Wages 12s per week; a wife and one child aged 15; he is a drunken, disorderly fellow and very much in debt.*

> *George Hall of Carr Bank, labourer. Wages 10s per week; he has reared ten children: he is in comfortable circumstances.*

> *George Locket of Kingsley (boatman), wages 18s per week, with a wife and seven children: his family are in a miserable condition.*

> *George Mosley of Kingsley (collier), wages 18s per week: he has a wife and seven children; he is saving money.*
> (Chadwick, op. cit., p. 206.)

Care of children

An exasperated clergyman once said that in his parish the children's worst enemies were their parents. All too often this was true. We read a lot about cruelty in factories and workshops, but the cruelty that went on in some of the houses was worse, as well as being more sustained, and much harder for the children to bear since it came from their own parents. The foreman of a cotton factory said that at the end of the day he often had to drive children from behind the store and among the cotton bales. He said he could not understand why they would not go home. Had he known more about their homes he would not have been so surprised.

In his *Sanitary Report* Chadwick said:

> *However defective many of the factories may be, they are all of them drier and more equably warm than the residences of the parent. It is an appalling fact that of*

Care of children

all who are born of the labouring classes in Manchester, more than 57 per cent die before they attain 5 years of age: that is, before they can be engaged in factory labour, or in any other labour whatsoever. (Chadwick, op. cit., p. 223.)

Parents did not give themselves a chance: they married young, and had far too many children. A visitor to Sedgley found that the people there usually married when they were very young and then had between six and twelve children. One working man in that town had thirty-six children. He married three times, and each of his wives bore him twelve children.

Too many people were not fit to be parents. If an adult wishes to spend all his money at the beginning of the week and then starve until the next pay-day, this is his business. It is a different matter if young children have to suffer as a result. To make it even worse, many parents squandered their money, not on food for the whole family, but on drink for themselves. There is a story of a mother and father who did no work. They sent their two children, aged twelve and eight, to the factory every day and then on Saturday night they took their wages, locked them in the cellar with a little tea and bread and then went out to get drunk. On Sunday morning they turned the children out into the streets to beg what they could for their breakfast.

Many mothers, although well-meaning, had no idea how to feed infants. Dr Lyon Playfair said: 'The greatest ignorance prevails as regards diet. It is not an uncommon thing to be consulted for emaciated children and find the food consists in great part of bacon, fried meat and fatty potatoes, when the infant has not, perhaps, two teeth in each jaw.' (State of Towns Commission, p. 68) Some miners killed their babies with kindness. When times were good they stocked their larders with all the things they liked – potatoes, bacon, fresh meat, sugar, tea and coffee.

Quaker soup kitchen. The Quakers did a great deal of charitable work, all of it very practical. They went among the people and saw to it that help went where it was needed.
Courtesy of *Illustrated London News.*

To them it seemed only right that the baby should have his share. The food he did not get was milk.

Children had no moral training. The example of its father and mother are the most important influences in a child's life, and these parents were often the worst of examples. They were coarse and vulgar; they spoke roughly and behaved badly. Probably the worst thing of all was the attitude that many parents had towards their children. When the children were young they were thought a nuisance; when they were older, they were looked on as a source of income.

A working mother would try to go back to the factory as soon as possible after her baby was born. She would perhaps leave the baby with its grandmother, with a low class baby-minder, or with another child. She might even lock it in a room on its own, or tie it to a table leg, and leave it all day. Slightly older children ran in and about the house, left entirely to themselves for hours together. There were often accidents, and in winter it was common for children to set their houses on fire and sometimes burn themselves to death.

To stop infants crying, or to keep small children from being a nuisance, some parents drugged them. There was a concoction called Godfrey's Cordial, which was a mixture of treacle, water and opium. The chemists made this up themselves, so the amount of opium in the mixture was a matter of chance. Another drug was a mixture of chalk and laudanum, called Atkinson's Infant Preservative. The parents would give their child some of this 'quietness' before going to work in the morning. They would give it another dose at lunch time and when they came home at night they would be too tired to put up with it, so they would drug it for a third time. Any baby that was drugged regularly like this soon died.

If a child survived, its parents would try to make what money they could from it. One way of doing this was sinister, though happily not very common. It was to enter a child into a burial club to which the parents paid a penny or twopence a week. Then, if the child died, they would draw burial money and as the funeral was cheap they made a profit. People would say to one another, 'That child will not live long. He is in the burial club.'

Of course, the usual way to make money from children was to set them to work, which is discussed in the chapter on child labour. All that need be said here is that, generally, the worst employer a child could have was his own father or mother. John Brooks of Hinckley said that the stocking-weavers there made their children of five work for ten hours a day. There is also a story from a Warrington pin factory where there was a foreman who was kind and considerate to all the children in his charge save two. He bullied them so savagely that one of the women workers reported him and the employer dismissed him. It turned out that it made little difference to the man how hard most of the children worked, but the two he bullied were his own and he took their wages for himself.

Amusements

Manchester was the first large industrial city outside London to have a park, although this was not until 1846. This gives us some idea of how difficult it was for the poor people of large cities to use their spare time pleasantly. People living in small towns and mining villages could walk into the country, but for many city dwellers the only playgrounds were the miserable alleys and courts where they lived. Even if the public parks and amusements had been there, working people would hardly have had the time to enjoy them. When trade was brisk they spent so long at work that they had no energy left for play. On top of this, people had no education, and no chance to use what little time they had at all intelligently. Too many could not even read, and for a lot more, reading was such hard work that it was no relaxation.

Descriptions of working people at leisure make rather depressing reading. This is what John Brooks said it was like in Hinckley.

> '*Are the people accustomed to any athletic games?*' '*No, there is no ground at all: if men or boys play, they must play on the highway.*'
> '*Are there any gardens accessible?*' '*None.*'
> '*No public walks?*' '*None, except the fields.*'
> '*How do people pass the Sunday?*' '*Those who inhabit the low districts either spend their time in courts exchanging fowls or bartering away their dogs, and so on, or in ranging the fields in the afternoon: after they have been lying a-bed, they take a stroll of three or four miles, come home weary and sleep away the afternoon.*'
> '*Do they usually go to the public house after their return from their rambles?*'
> '*I cannot say they do; they are very poor and cannot afford it, except in a few instances, where a poor man gets the earnings of his children: he might then go and spend them, but he must rob his children if he does. The general practice, is, on the Sunday evening, for those who are not able to make a decent appearance at a place of worship, to congregate together, pay their penny or half-penny and send for a newspaper from a public house.*' (State of Towns Commission p. 150.)

A visitor to Wolverhampton found Sunday there about as quiet. Most of the men were lounging around, dirty and unshaven, and just sucking at their pipes. The women stood in their doorways with their arms folded. No one could even be bothered to go for a walk. They had worked themselves until they were exhausted at the end of the week and now that they did have a day of freedom they did not know what to do with it. One group of five showed their whole attitude only too clearly. They were leaning over the wall of a pigsty, looking down, saying nothing, and the pigs were staring back at them.

A good, healthy activity some working men did have was gardening. They had no gardens to their houses, but near some towns there were allotments. William Hewitt gives us a long description of those at Nottingham. The plots were about 400 square yards in area, each with its own summer-house. A wealthier tradesman had his summer-house built of brick with a cellar and a kitchen. The ordinary workman might only have a wooden hut, but he did his best to make it attractive with rustic work or by training a hop or a pumpkin over it. They grew vegetables, soft fruits and apple trees, but an allotment was not just a plot of ground on which to grow food. With its summer-house and flowers, it was a place to relax on a Sunday or on a summer evening.

Unfortunately, not many towns were as lucky as Nottingham and even the

Nottingham allotments had their drawback: the rents. The owners were profiteers. Hewitt calculates that the 500 acres would have been let for normal farming at £1250 a year. As gardens, they brought in £6250, showing a profit of £5000. Each plot cost about £1 5s 0d a year, which was quite as much as the value of the fruit and vegetables the tenant could grow.

So far this account makes no mention of the one place of relaxation that the working man could find with no trouble at all: the public house.

Drinking

There were local fashions in drink, for example, whisky in Scotland and cider in some of the western counties. But over the country as a whole the two most popular alcoholic drinks were beer and gin.

Beer or ale has been made in this country for centuries. In the eighteenth century you could buy old, brown or pale ale. From 1720 there was also porter, a strong beer, nearly black in colour and heavily hopped so that it is very bitter. Guinness is a kind of porter. It is quite possible to be thoroughly drunk on beer; but beer is not nearly as harmful as gin, taken in large quantities.

Gin is a spirit distilled from grain and flavoured with the berries of the juniper tree. It came here from Holland – one name for it was hollands – and it became popular after 1690. In fact, it became altogether too popular and led to all the evils that Hogarth showed in his famous painting *Gin Lane*. Later in the eighteenth century gin-drinking was brought down to a more reasonable level, but gin was still cheap and easy to buy for many years.

Usually men were the worst drunkards. A report on Wolverhampton says that the locksmiths made themselves drunk on Saturday and most of Sunday. On Monday they found themselves without money, but they would still go to the public house hoping that the landlord would give them credit, or that someone would treat them.

Women often joined the men. Or, perhaps, a woman finding her husband had gone out drinking would send for a bottle of gin, call in her friend and the two would drink together. The woman did not always need the example of her husband. A London magistrate once had a visit from a father.

> *A decent man, a mechanic, waited upon me and asked my advice what he should do: he said, 'I have two daughters: one is only 16, the other is 14. My wife has taken to the habit of drinking, and all my Sunday clothes, my tools, and everything she can get hold of, goes to the pawn shop: all the children's clothes are taken whenever she can.'* (Parliamentary Papers, 1834, Vol. VIII, p. 15.)

It might be the whole family that went drinking. This was the scene outside a London public house one day in 1834:

> *A woman, almost in a state of nudity, with a fine infant at her breast, the only dress being its night-shirt, followed by another child about eight years old, a little girl without either shoes or stockings, followed a wretched-looking man into the house,*

73

and remained there some time: I saw them struggling through the crowd to get to the bar: they all had their gin: the infant had the first share from the woman's glass: they came back to the outside of the door, and there they could scarcely stand: the man and the woman appeared to quarrel: the little child in her arms cried: the wretched woman beat it most unmercifully: after waiting for a few minutes the other little child ran across the road: the woman called to it to come back: it did so and she beat it: and when the children made so much noise she could not pacify them, they all went into the shop again, and had some more gin, apparently to pacify the children. (Ibid., p. 35.)

Drunkenness, then, could affect the whole family.

There were a number of causes for drunkenness. The very condition of the homes and the streets explains a lot. The houses were filthy and overcrowded so that no one wanted to stay at home: but there were no parks, public libraries or decent places of entertainment if they went out. The public house with its lights and its warmth was the obvious place to go.

Certain social conventions made it difficult to avoid drink. Then, as now, people drank at weddings, christenings, and all kinds of parties: in addition, in those days you were expected to drink at work. Wheelwrights celebrated when they had put the iron tyre on a cartwheel, masons when they had laid a foundation stone, and carpenters when they had fitted the first joist in a house. When an apprentice black-smith started work, his mates turned him upside down and drove a nail through the sole of his shoe until he shouted 'Beer!' This meant he would buy drinks all round.

Sometimes publicans were in league with employers and they would arrange for the men to be paid in a public house. When the men came for their money they would have to wait, but if a crowd of men are idle in a public house it is fairly sure that they will buy drink. When the wages finally came the temptation to spend was great and wives often had to wait in the bar to make sure that their husbands gave them enough money for food.

All these causes – bad houses, lack of amusements, boredom and social conventions – were of long standing. Then, in 1830, Parliament passed the Sale of Beer Act. Wellington was Prime Minister at the time and he said that passing this Act was a greater achievement for him than winning the Battle of Waterloo. Until 1830 no one could sell drink unless he had a licence from the local Justices of the Peace. Now anyone could sell beer simply by paying a two guinea excise duty, and beer shops sprang up all over the place. Poor Law Guardians bought licences for paupers so that they could make a living; people would subscribe to buy a licence for a widow; tradespeople – blacksmiths, grocers, tailors – sold beer as a side line. Brewers did their best to help by buying a man a licence or advancing him beer on credit. By the end of 1830, 24 000 people had bought licences and by 1836 this number had risen to 46 000. In parts of some towns there was a beer shop or a public house for every twenty families.

Having more beer shops meant that people drank more beer, but it also meant, indirectly, that spirit drinking increased. The owners of the public houses found that they were losing trade to the new beer shops, and to win back their customers

Drinking

The public house.
This *Punch* cartoon
was intended to
show the evils of
allowing children
into public houses.
Reproduced by
permission of *Punch*.

they advertised their gin as much as they could. They also smartened up their houses so that they were brighter and more elaborate. The old-fashioned public house became a gin palace. They also employed musicians to come and play and even bought organs. Curiously, in Manchester, they used to play psalms on Sundays.

Drunkenness helped cause crimes of violence. In his evidence to the Committee on Drunkenness the Commissioner of the New Police, Sir Charles Rowan, pointed out that the professional criminals valued their wits too highly to dull them with

The Temperance Movement

drink, but constables and police magistrates told a different story. The constables had the task of arresting fighting drunkards and the magistrates sentenced them in droves.

However, poverty and misery were more important than crime. Families had little enough money for essentials, but the confirmed drunkard would see his family starve rather than go without drink. One day someone saw two men standing and talking together. Suddenly one of them pulled off his shirt, sold it to his friend and the two of them went into a public house to spend the money on drink. Even worse is the story of a woman who went to look for her husband and little girl. She found the man drinking, with his daughter shivering beside him. He had pawned her dress to buy gin.

Drunkenness was a scourge of the working classes. Too many of them lived in conditions that were foul: these conditions drove them to drink and this completed their ruin.

The Temperance Movement

Drinking was probably the worst of the working man's bad habits and the one that caused most distress to his family. To contest this there was a powerful temperance movement.

The early temperance societies were organised mainly by middle class people, and their members promised to be moderate in their drinking. They signed a paper, which became known as the 'moderate' pledge.

The Movement took a new turn in the 1830s with the conversion of Joseph Livesey, a cheese merchant from Preston. Livesey and his friends formed the Preston Temperance Society in 1832, which was different in two important ways from the earlier societies. In the first place, it was for ordinary working men, and in the second place its members believed, not in moderation, but in total abstinence. Livesey and his followers believed that alcohol was 'the devil in solution' so that it was quite wrong to have any of it at all, however small the quantity. It was a member of this society, Dicky Turner that gave the English language a new word. He was an enthusiastic total abstainer, but he had an unfortunate stammer. He stood up at a meeting and with his broad Lancashire accent said, 'I'll have nowt to do wi' this moderation botheration pledge: I'll be reet down and out tee-tee-total for ever and ever.'

From Lancashire the Temperance Movement spread all over the country. There were many temperance societies, who built temperance halls and set up temperance hotels. The Movement was a particular success in Cornwall, where its emblem was the temperance pig. People had piggy banks in which they put the money they would otherwise have spent on drink.

Temperance leaders realised the importance of education and in 1847 Jabez Tunnicliff of Leeds founded the Band of Hope. Many branches started, especially in Sunday Schools. They were popular with children because they organised visits, games and magic lantern shows. At these, slides in lurid colours showed what happened to a drunkard's inside. There were also Band of Hope choirs who sang temperance hymns:

The Temperance Movement

Sing a song of Saturday
Wages taken home
Ev'ry penny well laid out,
None allowed to roam!

Sing a song of Sunday,
A home that's black and bare,
Wife and children starving
A crust of bread their share.

Sing a song of Monday,
Brought before the 'beak',
Fine of twenty shillings,
Alternative 'a week'!

Workhouse for the children,
Workhouse for the wife!
Isn't that a hideous blot,
On our English life?

The Temperance Movement ran into a lot of opposition, even from the clergy. The members of the Church of England, in particular, were suspicious, for they could not accept the idea that alcohol was 'the devil in solution'. There are numerous references to wine in the Bible, and Christ himself drank it on many occasions. These included the Last Supper, which the Church continues to commemorate in the Communion Service, using alcoholic wine for the purpose. Temperance reformers explained away many of the Biblical references to wine — at least to their own satisfaction — but they had great difficulty with St Paul's advice to Timothy: 'Drink no longer water, but use a little wine for they stomach's sake and thine often infirmities.'

But in spite of opposition the Temperance Movement had some success. In 1834, Ralph Grindrod of Manchester, was the first doctor to be converted. There was a good deal of scientific controversy, and many odd experiments involving drunken animals, even water fleas. But the idea that alcohol was rarely good for sick people gained ground, and doctors prescribed it less and less.

Parliament, too, began to take notice. In 1837 it allowed a teetotal M.P., James Silk Buckingham, to head a Committee of Enquiry into drunkenness. This ended farcically because several of the Committee's proposals were impracticable. They suggested, for example, that there should be an end to the distillation of spirits, and the idea that there should be no whisky in Scotland seemed to M.P.s to be funny. They found plenty more reasons for merriment and poor Silk Buckingham saw his Report laughed out of the House of Commons. Later, however, there was a reaction. Parliament came to treat drunkenness as a serious problem and the result was a series of Acts which regulated the opening times of public houses and closed them altogether on Sundays in both Scotland and Wales.

The early Temperance reformers had so many quaint ideas that it is only too easy to laugh at them, but there is no doubt that drunkenness became less and less a problem as time went on. This was mainly due to improved conditions and greater opportunities for enjoying life in other ways than drinking. But the Temperance Movement must have its share of the credit.

ORIGINAL SOURCES

Balfour, Clara. *Morning Dewdrops, or the Juvenile Abstainer*. 1843. This is typical of temperance literature.
Chadwick, Edwin. *Report on the Sanitary Condition of the Labouring Population of Great Britain*. 1842.
Gaskell, P. *The Manufacturing Population of England*. 1833.
Kay, J. P. *The Moral and Physical Condition of the Working Classes*, 1832.
Report of the Commissioners for Inquiring into the State of the Large Towns and Populous Districts. Parliamentary Papers 1844.
Report of the Select Committee on Intoxication among the Labouring Classes (Inquiry led by James Silk Buckingham) Parliamentary Papers 1834 Vol. III.

FURTHER READING

Harrison, Brian. *Drink and the Victorians*. Faber, London, 1971. The history of our drinking habits.
Longmate, Norman. *The Water Drinkers*. Hamish Hamilton, London, 1968. An account of the Temperance Movement.

LITERARY SOURCES

Dickens, Charles. *Dombey and Son*. Penguin, Harmondsworth, 1970. (Chapter 38: engine driver's meal.)
Dickens, Charles. *Great Expectations*. Penguin, Harmondsworth, 1969. (Chapter 7: drunken father.)
Dickens, Charles. *Pickwick Papers*. Macmillan, Basingstoke, 1968. (Chapter 3: a drunkard's death; chapter 6: ill-treatment of a family.)
Dickens, Charles. *Reprinted Pieces*. Everyman's Library, Dent, London 1970. Sunday under Three Heads; As it is; problem of drink; As Sabbath Bills Would Make it. Criticism of Bill for Sunday observance.
Dickens, Charles, *Sketches by Boz*. Everyman's Library: Dent, London, 1968. (Scenes, chapters 5: life in Seven Dials; chapter 22: gin shops; chapter 23: drink.)
Gaskell, Elizabeth. *Mary Barton*. Penguin, Harmondsworth, 1970. (Chapter 4: a tea-party; chapter 10: ignorant wives.)

Working class discontent   8

THE MAIN CAUSES OF WORKING CLASS DISCONTENT HAVE BEEN COVERED IN DETAIL IN other chapters. Here we need only summarise them.

In the first place there were the problems connected with the trade cycle. During the boom most workers found jobs, and wages rose but prices tended to rise even more quickly. During the depression prices fell, but many workers could not take advantage of this because they were unemployed. 1826, 1837 and 1848, for example, were all years of widespread unemployment and distress.

There were also big variations in the price of bread, the staple food of working class families. Bad harvests from time to time brought high prices, and if these came during a depression, the poor suffered dreadfully. This was most frequent during the war when the general level of wheat prices was high, but it happened again in 1816 and in 1832, when there were bad harvests in years of depression.

Industrial changes brought problems: when a craftsman was trying to compete with a machine, he found himself in trouble. The handloom weavers have attracted the most attention, but men in many other trades suffered as well, for example the locksmiths of south Staffordshire.

The Poor Law of 1834 was another cause of discontent. The aim of this law had been to drive idle paupers to work by offering the workhouse as the only form of relief. During a depression, when there was mass unemployment and no hope at all of finding work, this was an added cruelty. To avoid starvation families had to split up, leave their homes and live in one of the hated 'Bastilles'.

Finally, the working men did not have any political power. There was no party in Parliament to represent them and they did not have the vote. There was no legal way at all to make Parliament change an old law, or make a new one, except to send in a petition. It was not usual for Parliament to pay much attention to petitions from working men, so it is not surprising that many of them became frustrated and tried to win their way by illegal means.

The working people reacted in many ways, and one of these was violence. Sometimes, but not very often, this was directed against particular people. In 1812 someone shot dead an unpopular Yorkshire manufacturer called William Horsfall. Blacklegs – people who go on working when their mates are striking – were very unpopular. In 1808 some weavers on strike invaded the homes of others who would not join them and took away their shuttles. In 1818 some Stockport strikers seized a number of girls who were going to work, and held them under a pump.

But it was much more common for workers to attack mills and destroy machinery. Many hand workers knew that machines were putting them out of business: they

Luddites

hated them, and often, in a blind fury, they destroyed them. In 1776 some spinners destroyed one of Arkwright's mills near Chorley, and all jennies in the area were smashed if they had more than twenty spindles. In 1818 there was an attack on a Stockport mill and troops had to come in to defend it. In 1826 over a thousand power looms were destroyed in the area around Blackburn and Bury.

These were more or less spontaneous uprisings, made with little planning or forethought, but there was also an organised campaign of destruction, carried on by people calling themselves Luddites. These took their name from Ned Ludd who, according to one story, was an apprentice who smashed his employer's equipment as revenge for a beating. More likely, no such person ever existed, 'Ned Ludd' being a name the workers made up and used when signing their threatening letters.

The Luddite movement began in the counties where stockings were manufactured — Nottinghamshire, Leicestershire and Derbyshire. There was no power-driven machinery in this trade, instead the weavers worked at home on small stocking frames. In the early nineteenth century their trade was already depressed because fancy hose had gone out of fashion, and so many people had taken up stocking weaving that the employers could pay low wages. They now made things much worse by bringing in a new type of wide frame, which produced a cheap, inferior stocking that brought prices down even further and wages along with them. The weavers banded together and went around at night, invading cottages where there were wide frames, and smashing them. By and large the weavers were successful and the masters had to meet their demands. This is a verse from a song called 'General Ludd's Triumph':

> The guilty may fear, but no vengeance he aims,
> At the honest man's life or estate,
> His wrath is entirely confined to wide frames
> And to those that old prices abate.
> These Engines of mischief were sentenced to die
> By Unanimous vote of the Trade:
> And Ludd who can all opposition defy
> Was the grand Executioner made.

In 1812 the movement spread to Lancashire, where the handloom weavers turned their wrath on the power looms. There were riots in Manchester, attacks on factories and widespread destruction of steam looms. Here and at Stockport there were secret committees who organised the movement. Each member took an oath of secrecy and also swore to help kill anyone who turned traitor.

The Lancashire Luddites were not as successful as those of the Midlands where the wide frames were scattered all over the countryside in cottages. Small groups of men could easily break into private houses. In towns like Manchester, however, the steam looms were in factories so that the workers had to attack them openly, in large bands. Troops could quite well defend the factories and it was fairly easy to recognise and arrest numbers of the rioters. Quite a lot were brought to trial, two of them were hanged and many more were transported.

In 1812 there was a Luddite rising in Yorkshire where the workers objected to shearing frames. Shearing is an important and highly skilled process in cloth finishing which was done by hand with large shears. Each of the new frames did the work of four men and so put many shearsmen out of work. When the employers refused to give up their frames the workmen began to destroy them. One of the most important attacks was on a mill at Rawfolds, belonging to William Cartwright. This has been described in Charlotte Bronte's novel *Shirley*. In Yorkshire the local military commander, General Maitland, kept the Luddites in check by sending small bodies of troops to patrol over a wide area, especially at night time. As in Lancashire, many rioters were arrested and fifteen men were hanged, three for the murder of Horsfall and the rest for attacking mills.

Another form of violence, but a very rare one, was the political plot. The most famous of these, the Cato Street Conspiracy of 1820, was organised by two men, Thistlewood and Edwards. Their plan was to murder several members of the Cabinet while they were at a dinner party. Unfortunately for the conspirators, Edwards was a government spy and he betrayed them. They were surprised in their hideout at Cato Street, and although Thistlewood killed one of his attackers and escaped, he was soon found and arrested. Petty little plots like these did a great deal of harm, since they gave the impression that there was a widespread conspiracy to organise something similar to the French Revolution in Britain. In fact, no such conspiracy existed. There was plenty of discontent, but the ordinary workers lacked the organisation to start a rebellion, and the educated people who were on their side — men like Cobbett and Hunt — did not want revolution, but reform.

Quite the opposite to violence was the attempt by the workers to win government help for their cause. They did this in two ways: one was to petition Parliament to make new laws, and the other was to work through the courts and see that they enforced old-fashioned laws that were in their favour.

In the early days of the Industrial Revolution a petition to Parliament was occasionally a success. In 1773 the silk weavers of Spitalfields in London won an Act for the regulation of their wages. In the City, wages were to be fixed by the Lord Mayor and the Aldermen, and in Middlesex and Westminster by the magistrates. The weavers welcomed this Act because they were no longer at the mercy of their employers. But as the Act only applied to the London area, many masters took their trade elsewhere. The weavers failed in their attempt to have the law applied all over England, and in 1824 Parliament repealed it.

But very few of these attempts to win help from Parliament had even this limited success. In 1808 the cotton weavers asked for a minimum wages Act, but Parliament turned them away and this was the usual fate of any plan to make a new law for the protection of workers.

However, there were already in existence some old laws which were to the advantage of the workers. One of these was the Statute of Artificers of 1562, which required anyone going into a trade to serve an apprenticeship for seven years, and controlled the number of apprentices that any master could employ. As the Act limited the number of men who could go into a trade, it tended to keep wages high.

The Statute of Artificers also allowed magistrates to fix minimum wages, and indeed every trade had its own rules and regulations, most of which, while they might have been useful in their day, were quite inappropriate at the time of the

Co-operative societies

Industrial Revolution. None the less, where these rules were to their advantage, the workers set about persuading courts of law to enforce them. In 1795 the men in the cloth-finishing trade prosecuted their employers for using a simple little machine called a gig mill, which had been made illegal in the reign of Edward VI, well over two hundred years before. These same men also joined with the weavers and tried to limit the number of looms that any one man could own, this again under a law of the sixteenth century. Similarly, the framework knitters of Leicestershire brought an action against an employer, Payne of Burbage, who was 'colting' – that is to say, employing too many apprentices.

But the workers did not find the courts of law at all sympathetic, and courts of law have their own ways of discouraging people who bring what they think to be frivolous actions. It was quite clear, for example, that Payne had done wrong and the court had to give judgement against him, but the judge awarded the stocking weavers only one shilling damages and ordered them to pay all the legal costs which ran into a considerable sum of money. This system of awarding only nominal damages, and then charging high costs was almost effective enough on its own, but Parliament also took a hand. One by one the laws which might have helped the workers were repealed – in 1809, for example, the laws forbidding the use of gig mills and limiting the number of apprentices in the wool trade, and in 1814 the Statute of Artificers.

The problem here was that during the Industrial Revolution trade and industry were expanding so rapidly that employers were highly impatient of anything that restricted them and prevented them from developing their businesses. They were in a far better position to influence Parliament than the workers. Further, economists like Adam Smith had put forward the doctrine of *laissez-faire* which means, simply, 'leaving alone'. They held that trade and industry would only develop if they were free from interference and control. The governments of the day accepted this point of view, so they were unsympathetic to the workers who wanted controls, and agreed with the employers who wished to see all restrictions abolished.

Quite a different way in which the working classes tried to help themselves was through the Co-operative Movement. This idea seems to have come mainly from the mill owner, Robert Owen. Owen was no ordinary manufacturer, but a man of vision who was on the side of the working classes and most anxious to improve their condition. Unlike the people who wanted to return to the old days, Owen saw that it was impossible to stop the growth of industry. He did want, however, to see that the wealth created by industry did not go to a privileged minority, but was shared by all. His aim was to change the whole order of society, and to set up 'villages of co-operation' in which everyone worked, not for themselves, but for the common good.

Owen found many enthusiastic followers. Co-operative societies were started in London and Brighton, and from here the Movement spread until by 1830 there were over three hundred societies. They opened shops with the idea of using the profits to help the Movement. There were co-operatives of producers, too, which were particularly popular with craftsmen who found their livelihood threatened by the new machines. To help these people the London Co-operative Society opened labour exchanges, which were not places where men went to find work but where,

Robert Owen. Owen was one of the great reformers of the period. As a factory owner he was a model employer, but later he attempted to reform society as he had reformed the New Lanark Mills. His visionary schemes for the trade union and Co-operative Movement failed and he is more famous for what he attempted than for what he achieved. Courtesy of Mansell Collection.

literally, they exchanged labour one with another. Workmen would bring in goods they had made and barter them with one another. There were valuers at the exchange who would assess the worth of anything that came in, and give the owner labour notes. The man could then spend his labour notes, like money, to buy goods brought in by others. The exchanges were a success for a while, during the early

Co-operatives

1830s, but soon their weaknesses began to show. They had to take anything that came, unlike a shop which can cut down or increase its orders to the wholesalers, just as it wishes. In times of glut their shelves were loaded with unwanted goods; in times of shortage they could not supply what was needed.

For Owen, and those who accepted all his ideas, co-operative shops and co-operatives of producers, were only the first stage towards setting up co-operative settlements. Owen was unable to interest Parliament in his scheme so he and his followers went ahead on their own. They set up several 'villages of Co-operation' the most important being Queenswood, or Harmony Hall as they called it, in Hampshire. This started in 1839 but had a short life, coming to an end in 1845.

The ideas behind the early Co-operative Movement were good enough, but they were not practical and the Owenite movement slowly died out. But just as it was dying, a group of people in Rochdale had a good idea – a co-operative shop which would return its profits to its customers in the form of dividends, paid out after all expenses had been met. These 'Rochdale pioneers' opened their store in 1844, and it was the first of the many co-operative shops which we know today. The Co-operative Movement of the second half of the nineteenth century came nowhere near to carrying out Owen's grandiose schemes – but it was practical, and so it succeeded.

We now come to the two things which, in the long run, have done most for the working classes – trade unions and political parties. The ordinary working man turned from one to the other, largely according to economic conditions. During a boom, the early trade unions were fairly effective. An employer does not like a strike

Trade union meeting. This cartoon shows the image the trade union movement had in the 1830s – slightly comical, but potentially dangerous. Courtesy of Mansell Collection.

at a time when trade is expanding, since he can sell his goods as fast as he can make them. Most strikes during a boom succeeded: the employers would meet the workers' demands in order to start production again as soon as possible. This gave the worker faith in his trade union, and he saw no reason to interest himself in politics. But after the boom would come depression and unemployment. Again the unions would call for strikes, but now employers were in a different mood. They had stocks in hand which they were unable to sell, so it did not worry them if their factories produced nothing for a time. Certainly they saw no reason to give way to demands to employ men whose wages they could not afford to pay. Strikes during a depression usually failed, and it was at this point that the working man lost faith in his union and turned to any political party that seemed to offer help. In 1819, which was a year of depression, the workers at the famous Peterloo meeting carried banners with political demands such as 'Vote by Ballot' and 'Equal Representation or Death'. The Reform Bill was passed in 1832, and this too was a year of depression so it was easy to persuade half-starved workers to riot for anything – even a Bill that was to do them no good at all. Further, as we shall see, the Chartists had their biggest following during two years of deep depression – 1842 and 1848.

During our period, this sporadic interest in politics went through three well-marked phases. English working class interest in the principles of the Radical Movement came with the French Revolution. After the war they were mixed up in the agitation that led to the Reform Act of 1832. Finally, there was the Chartist movement which began in the late 1830s and came to an end in the late 1840s.

A Radical is someone who wants to make sweeping changes. The Radical Movement began in the later part of the eighteenth century with such organisations as the Society of the Supporters of the Bill of Rights which was founded in 1769, and books like Tom Paine's *Common Sense*, which was inspired by the American War of Independence. Working class interest in the Radicals came with the French Revolution, when some of the more intelligent workers, the skilled artisans and tradesmen, formed themselves into Corresponding Societies. For example, in 1792 some London workmen formed the London Corresponding Society under the leadership of a shoemaker called Thomas Hardy. They organised themselves into groups of thirty which were to work for the reform of Parliament, and to press for the right to vote for all adult men. In addition, they exchanged letters from time to time with the revolutionary Jacobin clubs in France. At home they worked closely with middle class organisations like the Society of the Supporters of the Bill of Rights.

Soon, however, there was reaction. War with France broke out in 1793, so that anyone who approved of the French Revolution looked like a traitor to his country. Also the Reign of Terror in France made the Revolution look much less attractive. The government took action against the Radicals; Tom Paine escaped to France but many others were arrested and transported to Australia. Then in 1797 there was a naval mutiny at the Nore, followed in 1798 by a rebellion in Ireland. These two events had nothing to do with the Radical Movement, but they looked like part of a general plot to overthrow the Government. Parliament decided that all Radical organisations should end, so in 1799 they passed an Act making the Corresponding Societies illegal. Under this pressure the Radical Movement collapsed.

Chartism

It revived after the war when its leaders began, for the first time, to take notice of the factory workers. The journalist, William Cobbett, for example, wrote his 'Addresses to the Journeymen and Labourers' in his *Weekly Political Register* and in 1819 the mob orator, Henry Hunt went to St Peter's Fields, Manchester, to speak to some 80 000 people. But the most important movement which took place after the war was the agitation that led to the Reform Act of 1832.

The old House of Commons represented the landowners of the country, and very few other people besides. Tenant farmers, manufacturers and the middle classes generally felt that they too should have a say in the government of the country, so they started a campaign for a reform of Parliament that would allow them to have the vote. They made use of the discontent of the working classes and encouraged riots in London and Bristol which went a long way towards frightening Parliament into passing the Reform Act. This gave the vote to the middle classes, and allowed them to become Members of Parliament. However, it did nothing to help the working classes who found that the 'reformed' House of Commons had, if anything, even less sympathy for their welfare. The Radicals had wanted manhood suffrage and vote by ballot — but both were still a long way off.

The last of the working class political movements before 1850 was Chartism. This began in 1837 which was a black year for the ordinary working man. There was a bad depression so that there was mass unemployment and, to make matters worse, food prices were high. Also the working men realised for the first time just how unpleasant the new Poor Law was.

In the north a man called Feargus O'Connor took the lead and in 1837 founded the *Northern Star* newspaper, which put the point of view of the starving unemployed in the industrial towns. In London William Lovett and others formed the London Working Men's Association, and it was Lovett, Francis Place, and the Radical M.P., J. A. Roebuck, who drafted the charter which gives the movement its name. The charter was a document which set out a number of demands for the reform of Parliament. They were as follows:

Manhood suffrage. This meant that they wanted every man to have the right to vote. (It is interesting that at this time few people thought about giving women the right to vote.)

Vote by ballot. This would allow people to vote in secret and prevent intimidation at elections.

Annual Parliaments. This was to allow the electors to change their M.P.s at frequent intervals if they proved unsatisfactory.

Abolition of property qualification for M.P.s. This was to allow non-property owners to become Members of Parliament.

Payment of Members. This led on from the last point. As an M.P. had no salary in those days, he needed to be quite rich.

Equal electoral divisions. Before 1832 Cornwall had returned 44 M.P.s and the whole of Scotland only 45. Much had been done to put this right by the Reform Act, but there were still many places who returned too many M.P.s for their population, and others who returned too few.

Chartist riots at Newport, 1839. The failure of the Chartist Convention to persuade Parliament to meet its demands led the 'physical force' men in the party to organise a rebellion among the miners of South Wales. There was some bloodshed at Newport, but the rioters fled from a small body of troops without making a fight.
Courtesy of Mansell Collection.

The Chartists

Having stated their demands, the Chartists now set about seeing that they were met. In 1838 there were large meetings in many towns, with speeches and torch-light processions. In 1839 Chartist organisations all over the country sent representatives to London to meet in a Convention. They chose this name deliberately to frighten the governing classes – it was a reminder of the French Convention which had overthrown the King at the time of the Revolution. The Chartists looked on their own Convention as a rival to Parliament.

When the Convention met, it drew up a petition asking for the Charter to be made law. They claimed that 1 200 000 people signed this petition, but Parliament was not impressed and threw it out, by 235 votes to 45. The Convention was in difficulty: not only had the petition failed, but they were quarrelling amongst themselves. The 'physical force' men wanted a general strike, or even a rebellion, while the 'moral force' men still thought that they should try to win their way by persuasion. This rift caused the whole Convention to break up.

A few of the 'physical force' men did not give in so easily, and there was a rebellion in South Wales. It was a pitiful affair: thousands of miners advanced on Newport, but they fled before a tiny body of soldiers almost as soon as the first shot was fired. The main result of the rising was that it gave the Government the excuse they needed to arrest all the Chartist leaders they could, including Feargus O'Connor.

By the end of 1839 the failure of the petition, the break up of the Convention, the failure of the Newport rising and the arrest of their leaders all seemed to show that Chartism was dead. But Chartism, which had been born in one depression, revived in another. This was the year 1842 when there was a second petition to Parliament with, it was claimed, 3 750 000 signatures. Parliament was still not impressed and rejected the petition by 287 votes to 49. The Chartists organised protest meetings and there were many strikes, but again the Government took firm action. They sent troops who put down the disorders and hundreds of demonstrators were arrested. The strikes were failures, too, for they were held during a depression.

The Chartists now changed their tactics. They decided that they would build a new society on their own by making village settlements not unlike those planned by Robert Owen. The important difference was that in Owen's 'Villages of Co-operation' everything was owned in common, while in the Chartist settlements each family cultivated its own plot of land which it bought on the instalment plan. In 1845, to operate their scheme the Chartists formed a Co-operative Land Society which then bought several estates, the best known being Heronsgate near Rickmansworth. As a tribute to their leader they called it O'Connorville. In theory the Co-operative Land Society should have made a profit, but in fact it made a loss and came to an end in 1851. O'Connorville, however, survived for another twenty-five years as the tenants had bought their plots of land and were able to make a living from them.

The Chartists made their final effort in 1848, again a year of depression. They drew up their Third National Petition and decided that if Parliament rejected it they would call a National Assembly which would stay in session until the Charter was accepted. They decided to hold a mass meeting on Kennington Common, and march in procession to deliver their petition to Parliament. This petition, they claimed, had 5 700 000 signatures. The Government took fright, enlisted 150 000 special constables, brought troops and guns into London and summoned the aged Duke of Wellington to take charge. In the face of these preparations the great procession was a failure. The Chartists found the bridges over the Thames barred by soldiers with artillery, and they dispersed quietly. They put their petition in a humble cab and it went on to Parliament where it suffered the same fate as the two that had gone before. Chartism never recovered from this fiasco. It lingered on until the late 1850s, but after 1848 it counted for nothing.

These working class political movements, then, were not a success. The mass of the workers lacked education and organisation. In the early years they followed the lead of the middle classes who got what they wanted from the Reform Act of 1832 and then left the workers to struggle on their own. But probably the main cause of failure was a lack of interest. The working man only turned to politics when all else had failed; he only showed real concern during years of acute economic depression and when prosperity and full employment returned he could not be bothered with politics. It was nearly one hundred years after the failure of the Chartist movement before this country had a Labour government strong enough to rule according to socialist principles.

During our period, trade unions were more important than political parties, though that is not to suggest that they were particularly strong.

There had been trade unions of a kind during the eighteenth century, known as trade clubs, and due to poor communications they tended to be groups of men from one town or locality. They usually set up their headquarters in a public house, which explains such names as 'The Wheelwrights' Arms' and 'The Bricklayers' Arms'. They collected subscriptions, and used their funds to pay their members sickness or unemployment benefits; they could also use the money to finance a strike. They did not have large purses and it was as much as they could do to finance unemployment during a spell of bad trade, still less carry on a lengthy strike. What they could do was bargain with employers and they did indeed strike with some success when conditions were very favourable to them, for example, during a period of labour shortage.

During times of stress, such as mass unemployment, trade clubs in one or more counties might act together, but these wider organisations usually fell apart fairly quickly when the crisis was over.

It has been said that a proper trade union must represent workers in one trade, or group of allied trades, it must have a national organisation, and it must have a continuous existence. The eighteenth century trade clubs fulfilled only the first of these conditions.

A particular problem was that most trade union activities were illegal. At common law unions were 'conspiracies in restraint of trade' and any attempt to put pressure on an employer, or to organise a strike, was criminal. Fortunately for the unions the only remedy an employer had was by the clumsy procedure of common law indictment and by the time that had lumbered into action the offender was miles away. There was also a certain amount of statute law. Whenever the men in a particular trade became too difficult, Parliament would pass a law forbidding them to 'combine'.

During the Napoleonic Wars, working class organisations were suspect as the

Trade Unions

Government imagined they were sympathetic to the French Revolution. The Combination Acts of 1799 and 1800 substituted summary trials before magistrates for the long-winded common law process of indictment before a judge and jury. Action against the unions could now be swift and effective. How vigorously the law was applied is not clear: in some areas unions continued to work openly, though in others they were driven underground and became more like secret societies with elaborate initiation ceremonies involving swords, skulls and ritual oaths. The unions survived until 1824 when Parliament repealed the Combination Acts.

This was largely the work of the Radical leader, Francis Place. Not an M.P. himself, Place was helped in Parliament by a fellow Radical, Joseph Hume. Between them they managed to secure a Commission of Inquiry into the working of the Combination Acts. Place coached the witnesses and the Commission advised the repeal of the Acts.

Unions now began to multiply: in 1825 the Northumberland and Durham Colliers' Union was formed, followed in 1826 by the Journeymen Steam Engine Makers Union and in 1827 by the Friendly Society of Carpenters and Joiners. In 1829 John Doherty organised what was perhaps the first modern trade union – the Grand General Union of all the Operative Spinners of the United Kingdom. Another large union was the Operative Builders' Union, which was formed in 1832 by amalgamating many local unions of many different trades. At one stage this union had 60 000 members.

It was at about this time that Robert Owen began to take an active interest in the work of trade unions. As we have seen, it was Owen's aim to change society so that everyone could share in the prosperity brought by the Industrial Revolution and he thought that the trade unions might do much to help. Accordingly, he drew up a programme for the builders and presented it to them at their conference in 1833. He persuaded them to form themselves into a Grand National Guild which would take over the building industry. The Guild would employ all the workers there were in the building trade, undertake any work that had to be done and gradually force the employers out of business.

This was a grandiose scheme which was almost bound to fail, and indeed the end came quite soon in a way that was almost ridiculous. Combe, Delafield & Co., a firm of brewers, refused to employ union labour. By this time there was some measure of co-operation between trade unions and the building workers came to the help of the brewery workers by refusing to drink the beer of Combe, Delafield & Co., whereupon Cubitts, a large building firm, refused to allow any other kind to be drunk on their sites. The men went on strike and the masters retaliated by refusing to give a job to any member of the Operative Builders' Union. After a long struggle the employers won, and the big union fell to pieces. The masons were the first to break away, and the other trades followed. Some trades, like the carpenters and bricklayers, did manage to keep their national organisation but others, like the painters and plasterers, went back to having small local unions.

While all this was going on, Owen was making even more ambitious plans for the trade union movement. In 1833 he produced a scheme to amalgamate all the unions in the country into the Grand National Consolidated Trades Union, which was to take over the running of the country and supersede even Parliament itself. For a short time all went quite well, as many unions decided to affiliate with the Grand National, but soon there was trouble. In 1833 a group of Derby employers locked out their men, so the union had a major problem even before it was properly organised. It raised a levy from its members, but could not support the Derby workers for longer than four months. In 1834 several more strikes failed and Owen fell out with some of the trade union leaders. By the end of the year the Grand National had broken up, and Owen left the trade unions to their own devices while he concentrated on his 'Villages of Co-operation'.

High-flown schemes like Owen's were, and still are, beyond the reach of the trade unions. But how successful were they in their more practical work of bargaining with employers for more pay and better conditions?

Some evidence is provided by the story of two strikes in the Northumberland and Durham coalfield. Here the men had quite a number of complaints. They had to enter into a yearly bond to work for the same employer for a fixed wage, but the employer only undertook to find three days' work in any one week. There was also a system of fines to penalise men who sent up corves containing stone mixed with the coal. This was fair in principle, but the men were sure they were being fined when they should not have been. Nor were the miners sure of keeping their homes. The house went with the job, and if the employer did not take on a man at the yearly binding, then he would put him out of his cottage. The miners also felt that boys worked too long hours.

In 1830 these miners had formed a union under the leadership of a man called 'Tommy' Hepburn, and in 1831 they went on strike. The strike went on for several weeks and in the end the employers gave way on a number of points. They raised the minimum wage by one shilling a week, they limited the boys' hours to twelve a day and they changed the system of fines to the men's advantage.

But the following year it was the employers' turn to start a dispute. They refused to sign on men unless they left the union, they evicted strikers from their homes, and they brought in lead miners to work the coal pits. The coal-miners attacked these blacklegs viciously and some of them assaulted a magistrate who died soon afterwards. The authorities met violence with violence, and the employers stood firm. Miners in pits that had gone on working paid a levy to help their comrades on strike, but they soon got tired of this and refused to pay any more. The strikers had to accept the employers' demand to dissolve their union, and even Hepburn accepted work in return for a promise not to join a trade union.

Why did the men succeed in 1831, while in 1832 they failed?

1831 was a boom year. There was full employment, and production of nearly all goods, including coal, was at a peak. The pit owners could sell all the coal they produced, and if they lost a day's work, they lost money. It is not surprising that they gave in to the men; it was well worth their while to let them have their way in order to get them back to work. 1832, however, was a year of acute depression. The price of coal was falling, and it was difficult to sell. Pit owners had large stocks in their yards that no one would buy, so it mattered little to them whether the miners were working or not. As a result they were quite ready for a fight to the finish, and did not give up until they had smashed the miners' union. This was the general pattern in all trades. If there was a boom strikes were likely to succeed; if there was a depression strikes were likely to fail.

However, the trade union movement was the most hopeful cause for the working man. Owen's grand schemes had come to nothing and strikes were only likely to succeed in times of prosperity. But on the other hand many of the little Trade Clubs had developed into large unions, some of them with a national organisation and already able to bargain with employers on equal terms. The movement was probably the better for shedding its wilder dreams and coming to terms with reality. In the middle years of the nineteenth century the skilled workers grouped themselves into compact unions; they were well organised and were made up of men whose services were essential to their employers. Such unions were a success, and in the later years of the century many unskilled workers, such as the dockers, were able to follow their example and form effective unions.

We shall now see what the governments of the day thought and did about working class discontent.

In the eighteenth century most working people were farm labourers or craftsmen in small towns. Large cities with their masses of factory workers were quite new, and quite frightening, especially as they began to appear at about the same time as the French Revolution. The first reaction was to try to stamp out discontent.

We have already seen that the Radical Movement was suppressed during the war. We have also seen that Parliament refused to listen with any sympathy to petitions from working men, and repealed laws like the Statute of Artificers that were to their advantage. They went even further and made new laws that were intended to hamper the workers in their attempts to improve their lot.

In the first place, they tried to make it difficult to form trade unions, and we have already seen how this culminated in the passing of the Combination Acts of 1799 and 1800.

Secondly, there were attempts by the government to silence their political opponents among the working classes. After Peterloo in 1819, during a trade depression and when there was widespread discontent, Parliament passed what were known as the Six Acts. Opponents called them the Gag Acts. They were as follows:

Magistrates had more powers to deal with offenders.
Drilling and arms training were made illegal, which was hardly unreasonable!
The laws against seditious libel were made more severe.
Magistrates were given the right to search houses and confiscate any weapons they might find.
The right of public meeting was restricted.
Periodicals were to pay the same tax as newspapers.

The Combination Acts and the Six Acts were the most notorious measures passed at this time, but there was a whole series of Acts aimed at putting down discontent. As magistrates and judges were as frightened as the government they often enforced the new laws vigorously. After a weavers' strike in Manchester sixty-six men were charged with rioting and destroying machinery; ten of them were transported for life and thirty-three imprisoned. But the most famous case was that of the Tolpuddle Martyrs in 1833.

A group of farm labourers from Tolpuddle in Dorset decided to form a trade union. Their leader was George Loveless. As was quite usual in those days they had an initiation ceremony at which the members took an oath. The local magistrates took fright when they heard of this, so they warned men against joining the union and arrested Loveless and five other ringleaders. The Combination Acts had been repealed in 1824 but in 1797, after the naval mutiny at the Nore, Parliament had passed an Act against taking illegal oaths. This law, which had been intended to put down mutinous seamen, was now used against Loveless and his friends. Judge and jury both disliked them so at their trial they received the thoroughly unreasonable sentence of seven years' transportation. The Government then hurried them off to Australia, before the public fully realised what had happened. There was so much agitation that the men had a free pardon, but this was not until 1838 by which time they had served most of their sentences.

To back up the magistrates the Government used soldiers. We have already seen how General Maitland used his troops to put down the Yorkshire Luddites. The war gave the government an excellent excuse: it could say the country needed troops to keep out the French, which it did, but those same troops could also put down riots and disperse meetings. Two new forces were raised: the Volunteers, who were infantry, and the Yeomanry, who were cavalry. Members of the Yeomanry were usually quite wealthy; they were the people who most mistrusted the working classes and were particularly keen to go into action against the mobs. They caused many fights, the most notorious being the Peterloo incident of 1819. This took place at St Peter's Fields near Manchester, and they named the affray after this and the famous battle of 1815. A crowd, said to number 80 000, came to listen to the radical speaker Henry Hunt. The meeting was quite orderly, but a body of Yeomanry cavalry appeared and charged the crowd, trampling and sabreing men, women and children alike. Eleven people died and hundreds more were injured. The reaction of the Government was to congratulate the magistrates who ordered the charge and pass the six Acts.

Even more sinister was the use of government spies. These men wormed their way into working class organisations by pretending to sympathise with them, and then reported what they discovered to the magistrates. Sometimes they went even further than this. If a spy is to earn his rewards he must find someone to report. This is a problem if there is no-one doing wrong, so a spy would encourage a man to break the law, and then report him. For example, two spies disguised as militiamen one day went to a quite innocent man called James Starkey and asked him the best way to blow up a mill. 'I would use a barrel of gunpowder', he said, and thought no more about it. The next day he found himself under arrest for inciting two of the militia to blow up a mill. He was let off, but others were not so lucky. In 1817 the spy Oliver actually managed to stir up a half-hearted rebellion in Derbyshire. As a result of this twenty-three men were arrested for high treason, and three of them were hanged.

But active hostility on the part of the government declined. Although the fear of revolution did not end with the war in 1815, it began gradually to die away.

Working class discontent

People realised that it was only in places where spies had been active that there had been talk of rebellion. With growing confidence came growing toleration, and in 1824 Parliament repealed the Combination Laws, so clearing the way for the free development of the trade unions. As we have seen, it was the trade unions which offered most hope to the working man.

ORIGINAL SOURCES

Cole, G. D. H. and Filson, A. W. *British Working Class Movements – Selected Documents 1789–1875.*
Owen, Robert. *The Life of Robert Owen, Written by Himself.* 1858.

FURTHER READING

Hammond, J. L. and Hammond, Barbara. *The Skilled Labourer 1760–1832.* Longman, London, 1919.
Hammond, J. L. and Hammond, Barbara. *The Town Labourer 1760–1832.* Longman, London, 1966.
Marlow, Joyce. *The Tolpuddle Martyrs.* Deutsch, London, 1972.

LITERARY SOURCES

Bronte, Charlotte. *Shirley.* Collins, London, 1952. (Chapters 2 and 19: Luddites.)
Disraeli, Benjamin. *Sybil.* World's Classics Series, O.U.P., Oxford. (Chapter 12: a crowd attack on a manor house, based on the 1842 Chartist strikes and riots.)
Gaskell, Elizabeth. *Mary Barton.* Penguin, Harmondsworth, 1970. (Chapters 15 and 16: a strike.)
Gaskell, Elizabeth. *North and South.* Penguin, Harmondsworth, 1970. (Chapter 10: class struggle; chapters 17, 19 and 22: a strike.)

Crime 9

THE GROWTH OF TRADE AND INDUSTRY DURING THE INDUSTRIAL REVOLUTION HELPED to cause an increase in crime. In the first place, people had more money and more goods so there was more temptation to steal. Secondly, many towns were now so big that criminals could vanish into the crowd and be anonymous. In the villages and little market towns everyone knew everyone else and a criminal did not have much chance; but in the big cities it was quite different. Thirdly, the industrial changes unsettled society: people moved to new homes, in places where they had neither friends nor relations. Their economic life was not secure; from time to time there was unemployment, and always there was poverty. Writing in 1796, a magistrate called Patrick Colquhoun said of London:

> Twenty thousand individuals rise every morning without knowing how or by what means they are to be supported through the passing day, and in many instances, where they are to lodge on the succeeding night. (Patrick Colquhoun, Police of the Metropolis, p. 33.)

Another thing that encouraged crime was the system for conducting a prosecution. Today the police do all the work of bringing a criminal to justice, but in the eighteenth century if you wanted someone punished you had to bring the case against him yourself. Many people found it better to let a criminal go unpunished than go to all the trouble and expense that this involved. Even if a prosecutor decided to go ahead it was quite likely that friends of the accused would threaten him and frighten him into changing his mind.

Probably one of the most fruitful causes of crime was the shortage of efficient police. If anything prevents a man from doing wrong, it is the threat of being caught, but the eighteenth century criminal knew that it was most unlikely that anyone would catch him. Under these conditions crime flourished.

By now the river Thames was thick with shipping. Cargoes worth thousands of pounds were discharged every day, and thieves took their toll. There were no docks so the ships were unloaded into lighters by men called dumpers and scuffle-hunters. They stole so regularly that they looked on their perquisites almost as a right. To take sugar a man would hang a thin sack from his shoulder, hiding it under his waistcoat, 'exhibiting to the superficial observer only the appearance of the natural protuberance of the belly'. Otherwise, they took it away in their hats or their pockets.

Theft

Sometimes the thieves worked with 'mud-larks'. These were children who poked around in the river mud at low tide looking for bits of wood, coal, nails, or anything which might have fallen in the water. These were only too glad to catch small packets of sugar, and coffee, thrown from a ship, and take their share of the profits. Watermen were more ambitious. They took not only packets of sugar and coffee, but kegs of rum, sacks of wheat and bales of cotton. The dumpers used to pass these goods through the scuttles and portholes.

The most ambitious plundered at night, even working the cranes to take what they wanted. There were gangs of water pirates who would take over a ship and steal by force. One such gang weighed a ship's anchor and stole the cable. When the captain caught them in the act and asked what they were doing they told him, bade him good morning and just rowed away. There was nothing he could do to stop them.

Stealing was common from the dockyards. Workmen would take nails, bolts, timber, cordage and sailcloth. Clerks and storemen practised fraud: for example, when old stores were offered for sale they would add some new ones and pocket the money themselves. A clerk's salary was between £30 and £40 a year – but there were people willing to pay £300 to have one of these jobs, because of the chances of making money dishonestly.

According to Colquhoun, burglary and highway robbery were usually the work of men discharged from prison and the hulks, who had learnt the trade inside. They would watch a house for days before breaking in, so that they knew the habits of the family. If they were lucky, they would have the help of a servant who would tell them exactly where the valuables were – discharged servants would often do this to take their revenge.

Servants were also useful to highwaymen, since they would know when their employers were going out carrying valuables. Highwaymen and footpads were often violent. As Colquhoun says, 'their outrages are too often marked with those acts of cruelty and barbarity which justly render them objects of dread and terror'.

Around London, farmers were often the victims of robbers, who took flour, corn, potatoes and poultry, which they disposed of quickly and easily in the city. They also took cattle, always being careful to make an arrangement with a dishonest butcher, who would kill and skin the beasts at once, so that they could not be recognised.

There is one interesting link, and a very direct one, between the growth of one particular industry and a crime. Birmingham manufacturers were developing their metal trades at this period, and a man who could turn out imitation silver buttons found he could do quite a good job at turning out imitation silver coins. Colquhoun says:

> Fraudulent die-sinkers are to be found both in the Metropolis and in Birmingham, who are excellent artists, able and willing to copy the exact similitude of any coin from the British guinea to the sequin of Turkey or to the Star Pagoda of Arcot. (Ibid., p. 114.)

They even counterfeited copper coins. They used pure copper, just like the mint, but they cut down the weight. The best profit was in farthings, because it was possible to make them very thin without anyone noticing.

These, then, were some of the activities of the professional master criminals. To it we must add a mass of petty crime, mainly thieving and violence, which was mean, unpleasant and uninteresting.

How did society try to protect itself from the criminal?

The Police in the eighteenth century

The police system had been growing in a haphazard way since the Middle Ages. The people in charge were the magistrates, which today would seem very odd. It is not good that the men responsible for bringing criminals to justice should also be responsible for trying them. But until proper police forces were established, from 1829 onwards, the magistrates had important police duties. When a criminal was arrested he went to a magistrate's house for questioning, not a police station. It was also the duty of the magistrates to appoint constables and to see that they did their work. This, of course, is one of the functions of a Chief Constable today.

Magistrates were unpaid amateurs with so many demands on their time that they could not have done all their work well, even if they had tried. Many were conscientious men who did their best; many more were content to get through their work with a minimum of effort and were not too worried about how efficient they were. A few were positively corrupt, especially in London. These were the notorious 'trading justices', who gave judgement according to the bribes they received, and made up to £1000 a year in this way.

Under the magistrates came the constables. The constable is first mentioned in 1252 when Henry III issued a writ for the enforcement of the Assize of Arms. A constable was to be appointed in any place that did not have a mayor, reeve or bailiff, and he was to have the duties of raising the hue and cry, which meant organising the pursuit of criminals, and of keeping watch and ward, which meant organising the policing of his town or village. In the eighteenth century, we find that the constable's duties included patrolling their areas once a day and visiting public houses every week 'to see that no unlawful games are permitted and that labouring people are not suffered to lounge and tipple until they are intoxicated'. constables were unpaid, and appointed only for one year. It was an unpopular job and anyone who could afford to, paid someone to do the work for him. Not many of these substitutes were at all efficient.

Sometimes the constable had headboroughs to help him. In the Middle Ages it had been the practice to put men into groups of ten, called tythings. If any member of the tything committed a crime then the other nine had either to deliver him for punishment, or, if they let him escape, pay the penalty themselves. The headborough was the man in charge of the tything. By the eighteenth century this idea of the collective responsibility of the tything no longer worked, but in many places there were still headboroughs and they did the work of deputy constables.

These three officials, the magistrate, the constable and the headborough, were legacies of the Middle Ages. As time went on they were found to be inadequate, especially in the big towns, including London. Accordingly, many towns supplemented their amateur officials by having paid watchmen. In 1663, for example, the London authorities set up one such force. This was in the reign of Charles II, so the new watchmen were called 'Charleys'.

Police in the eighteenth century

Generally speaking, watchmen were not efficient. Wages were as low as $8\frac{1}{2}d$ a night, and none were paid more than 2s. Colquhoun says:

> The encouragement being, in many instances, so small, few candidates appear for such situations, who are really, in point of character and age, fit for the situation. The managers have, therefore, no alternative but to accept of such aged and often superannuated men, living in their respective districts as may offer their services: this they are frequently induced to do from motives of humanity, to assist old inhabitants who are unable to labour at any mechanical employment, or perhaps with a view to keep them out of the workhouse. (Ibid., pp. 213–4.)

Criminals found it easy enough to bribe men like this, and even easier to frighten them.

During the eighteenth and early nineteenth centuries, some towns in the provinces set up improved Watch Forces, which were police forces in all but name. There were also some interesting developments in London. These began in Henry Fielding's office in Bow Street. Henry Fielding was a magistrate who was determined to do all he could to put down crime and no criminal brought before him had any hope of gain from threats or bribery. But he realised that good law courts were only a start, and that something must be done to bring as many criminals as possible to justice. Accordingly, in 1748 he gathered together a group of men who had proved themselves as efficient parish constables, and suggested they should form a body to be known as the Bow Street Runners. He could offer them no salary at first, but they were able to make money since it was then the practice to give rewards for arresting criminals and prosecuting them successfully. Also the Runners soon found they could make a good living by acting for part of their time as private detectives. Because they were detectives, Runners did not wear uniform, though each one carried a small staff, a few inches long, with a crown on the end. This was the same as was carried by constables as their emblem of authority.

Henry Fielding died soon after this, in 1754, but his blind half-brother, John, carried on the work. He too was a fearless and incorruptible magistrate, and he too was interested in police matters. In addition to the Runners he set up two groups of uniformed police for patrol work. These were the Bow Street Horse Patrol and the Bow Street Foot Patrol. Part of their uniform was the famous scarlet waistcoat, which gave them the nickname 'Robin Redbreasts'.

Bow Street was a success, so much so that in 1792 Parliament passed the Middlesex Justices Act. This set up seven London Police Offices modelled on those in Bow Street. Each had three magistrates drawing salaries of £400 a year and six constables earning 12s a week. The Act meant that the 'trading justices' could be taken from their duties, while the forty-two constables were a useful reinforcement for the Bow Street Runners. In 1800 another Act set up a Police Office to deal with crime on the River Thames.

These then, were the organised police forces. They were obviously quite inadequate for their task, and in despair the authorities and private individuals tried to check crime in other ways.

One particularly unfortunate method was by giving rewards. Up to £40 would be paid to anyone who secured the arrest of a criminal and prosecuted him success-fully. There were several things wrong with this system. Innocent people found themselves accused of crimes and convicted by perjury, so that their accusers could have a reward. Often a promising young criminal would be allowed to get away – if arrested before he had done anything serious, the reward would be small. It would be better to wait until, as they put it, he 'weighed £40'. A man called Vaughan who was a member of the Bow Street Horse patrol actually organised a burglary so that he could make an arrest and collect his reward.

Sometimes private individuals would join together. They might do as the citizens of Leicester did and give money so that the city could have extra watchmen; they might raise a small private police force of their own to patrol their part of the town. As we have seen, it was difficult to secure a conviction, so many towns formed Associations for the Prosecution of Felons in order to save any one individual the worry and expense of bringing a criminal to justice. All these duties, of course, should belong to the police, and it was quite wrong that the burden should fall on ordinary citizens.

Yet another way in which they attempted to check crime was by making punish-ments severe. By the end of the eighteenth century there were over two hundred capital offences. This defeated its own purpose, since many judges and juries refused to convict criminals for small offences because they knew the punishment was death. Stealing goods worth more than 40s was punishable by hanging, so that if a jury took pity on a prisoner, they would swear that what he had taken was worth only 39s whatever its true value. This was known as pious perjury.

One great weakness with the idea of savage punishments is that it takes no account of the way a criminal's mind works. It is not the fear of punishment that keeps a man from doing wrong: it is the fear of being caught.

Police reform

We have already seen that there was some measure of reform in the eighteenth century. This began with the work of the Fieldings at Bow Street and was carried further by the Middlesex Justices Act of 1792. But these reforms, good enough in themselves, were only a beginning. People like Colquhoun saw that the only good answer was a properly organised police force, and in London there were several attempts to create one. But there was much opposition to this idea. In 1785 there was a bill to set up a police force for London, but it was attacked by the Lord Mayor and Aldermen as 'the entire subversion of the chartered rights of the greatest city in the world, overturning the forms established by the wisdom of our ancestors, and setting up a system of police altogether new and arbitrary in the extreme'. (J. F. Moylan, *Scotland Yard*, p. 25.)

Similarly, in 1822, a Parliamentary report on the London police said it was impossible 'to reconcile any effective system of police with that perfect freedom of action and exemption from interference which is one of the greatest privileges and blessings of this country'. (Moylan, op. cit., p. 26.) People thought that it was better to have criminals rather than police, because police would be a threat to the Englishman's freedom, while the criminals were not.

Police reform

A man who disagreed most vehemently with this was Sir Robert Peel. As Chief Secretary for Ireland he had already organised a police force for that country in 1814, and he was anxious to try his ideas in England. He had his chance when he became Home Secretary in Wellington's Government in 1828. He at once persuaded Parliament to appoint yet another committee on the police of London, and this one reported in favour of a properly organised force. Peel then prepared the Metropolitan Police Improvement Bill, which passed both houses of Parliament and became law in 1829.

Under this Act there were to be two Commissioners of Police to administer the area that had been covered by the Bow Street Foot Patrol. Its boundary ran between four and seven miles from Charing Cross. The Commissioners had no authority beyond that boundary, nor did they have any control over the City of London. But within this area the Act swept away the Bow Street Foot Patrol, the constables and watchmen, and removed from the magistrates all their police duties. The first two Police Commissioners were Sir Charles Rowan, who had been a colonel in Wellington's army, and a young barrister, Richard Mayne. It was obviously a good idea to have a soldier and a lawyer to organise the new police force: one had the experience of training and controlling large bodies of men, while the other could interpret the law and draw up regulations.

Rowan and Mayne divided their area into seventeen divisions, and in each division there was a company of police. In charge of each company there was a superintendent who had four inspectors to assist him. Each inspector had four sergeants, while each sergeant had nine constables, making a total of 144.

The aims of the new police were set out in a book of instructions:

> It should be understood at the outset that the principal object to be attained is the Prevention of Crime.
>
> To this great end every effort of the Police is to be directed. The security of person and property, the preservation of the public tranquillity, and all the other objects of a Police Establishment, will thus be better effected, than by the detection and punishment of the offender, after he has succeeded in committing the crime. This should constantly be kept in mind by every member of the Police Force, as the guide for his own conduct. Officers and Police Constables should endeavour to distinguish themselves with such vigilance and activity, as my render it extremely difficult for any one to commit a crime within that portion of the town under their charge. (Charles Reith, *A New Study of Police History*, p. 135.)

Prevention of crime is still the first duty of the police, although no one in charge of a force today would carry the idea as far as Rowan and Mayne did. They even refused to have detectives.

Many of the new police were former soldiers, especially superintendents and inspectors. Superintendent May, for example, had been a sergeant-major. A good number of the rank and file had been privates in the army.

Pay was not generous. A constable had 21s a week, which was about average for an ordinary worker in those days; but skilled men in industry could earn 30s a week, so good recruits for the police were rare. Of the first 2800 who enlisted, the vast majority left the force before long, well over half of them being dismissed for coming drunk to their duty.

Following the establishment of the New Police there were several important developments. In the first place, the police went some way towards winning the confidence of the public. At first, most people distrusted them completely. This kind of leaflet was distributed from time to time:

> *Liberty or Death! Britons!! and Honest Men!!! The Time has at last arrived. All London meets on Tuesday. We assure you that 6000 cutlasses have been removed from the Tower for the use of Peel's Bloody Gang. These damned Police are now to be armed. Englishmen, will you put up with this?* (Ibid., p. 155.)

Army officers incited their men to attack the constables, there were quarrels with firemen and rich people disliked them since they attempted to control traffic. Some noblemen instructed their coachmen to use their whips on policemen, or even to run over them. Most serious of all was the hostility of the magistrates who quite often sided with criminals against the police, and gave the lightest sentences they could. The reason the magistrates felt so strongly was because Peel's Act had taken away their police duties, and so cut down their authority.

In the face of this, Rowan and Mayne were very restrained, and they instructed their men to behave in the same way. The constables' instructions said:

> *He will be civil and attentive to all persons, of every rank and class: insolence and incivility will not be passed over. He must remember that there is no qualification more indispensable to a Police Officer than a perfect command of temper, never suffering himself to be moved in the slightest degree, by any language or threats that may be used: if he do his duty in a quiet and determined manner, such conduct will probably induce well-disposed by-standers to assist him should he require it.* (Ibid., p. 140.)

After a time this policy began to work. People gradually became used to the sight of the peeler in his stove-pipe hat, and realised that he was not there to plague honest citizens. Dislike of the police declined, though with a certain section of the public it has never quite vanished even today.

Peelers. The earliest photograph of the Metropolitan Police. They have their wide leather belts and 'stove-pipe' hats. Their collars were so high that it was said, as a joke, that a man could not turn his head without turning his whole body. By kind permission of the Metropolitan Police.

101

The Metropolitan Police

There were important changes in 1839 when Parliament passed the Metropolitan Police Act. The area the Metropolitan Police had to control was extended so that it included everything within about fifteen or sixteen miles of Charing Cross. This was the ground that the Bow Street Horse Patrol had covered. The Horse Patrol itself was included in the New Police and became the nucleus of the mounted branch. Secondly, the Bow Street Runners were disbanded, as were the constables attached to the courts set up by the Middlesex Justices Act of 1792. Finally, the New Police absorbed the Thames Police.

The effect of this Act was, then, to give the New Police a much bigger area to manage, and to give them absolute control within that area. It was a tribute to their success. The Act of 1839 had one unfortunate result, however. Now that there were no Bow Street Runners and no constables attached to the Magistrates' Courts, there were no detectives at all in the Metropolitan area. Rowan and Mayne did nothing about this for some time. They were obsessed with the idea that the work of the police was to prevent crime, and so they saw little point in having detectives. There was also strong public feeling against policemen in plain clothes – they were too much like the government spies described in the last chapter. A police constable named Popay did not make matters easier by behaving like a spy. He pretended to join a group of agitators, and encouraged them to be violent in the hope of making some arrests. When he was found out, the public was furious.

But opinion swung the other way when the police bungled the capture of a vicious criminal called Daniel Good, and somewhat reluctantly, Rowan and Mayne appointed two inspectors and six sergeants to do detective work. This was a minute force, and there were not to be many detectives at Scotland Yard until after Rowan and Mayne had died. Rowan died in 1852, but Mayne lived until 1868. To the end, they held that the duty of the police was to prevent crime, and that the very fact that you had to use detectives was an admission of failure.

· The Metropolitan Police was the model for all the provincial borough forces. In 1836 there was a Royal Commission to look into the problem of setting up rural police forces. It included Edwin Chadwick and Colonel Rowan. With Chadwick guiding the proceedings it is not surprising that the Commission advised strong central control of the proposed county forces, but in the event Parliament passed a much more modest measure. This was the County Police Act of 1839, which allowed the magistrates in quarter sessions to appoint a Chief Constable whose duty it would be to organise a force. But there was no obligation; if the magistrates felt they did not want a police force in their county, they did not have to have one. By 1853, twenty-two counties had adopted the Act. Then in 1856 Parliament passed the Rural Police Act, and this made it compulsory to have a police force in all counties. To soften the blow, the Act said that the government would pay one-quarter of the cost of every force, provided that their Inspector's report on it was satisfactory.

Prisons in the eighteenth century

Descriptions of two prisons by the famous reformer, John Howard, will set the scene for us:

County Bridewell, Wymondham: A day room, with three closets on one side of it, for night rooms, about six feet by four. A prisoner complained to me of being obliged to lie in one of these closets, with two boys who had a cutaneous disorder. There is another room for women, in which, at my visit in 1779, there were four dirty and sickly objects at work with padlocks on their legs, though they were never out in the court except on Sunday. The very small quantity of straw on the floor was worn almost to dust. There is a dungeon down eight steps with the stocks in it. It is 15½ feet by eight, and six feet high: now arched with brick: a dirt floor: has two apertures at the top of a foot diameter. Neither the rooms nor the court secure. Prisoners in this bridewell are not only confined within doors, but generally in irons. (J. Howard, *State of the Prisons*, pp. 200–1.)

County Gaol at Warwick: The felons were sadly overcrowded. Only one small Day room for the men: I saw 32 lay chained in a dungeon of 22 feet diameter, down 32 steps, two of whom were ill of a slow fever. There were three others in a room, very ill and in irons. In two rooms, (7½′ × 6′) with apertures only in the doors, there lay 14 women, almost suffocated. From the apertures of this dungeon, the steam of the prisoners' breath comes out, in winter, like the smoke of a chimney. (Ibid., p. 203.)

What is the purpose of a prison? Today, most members of the prison service would say that their work is to reform criminals and make good citizens of them. Many members of the public would say that going to prison is a punishment for committing a crime. In the eighteenth and early nineteenth centuries there was no attempt at all by the prison authorities to reform criminals in what were known as common gaols, nor were the prisons places for punishment. In the main they were not for criminals at all, but for debtors and most of the criminals in them were either waiting to be tried, or, if they had been found guilty, they were waiting for some form of punishment other than imprisonment. This could be hanging, transportation or being sent into the army or navy. For minor offences the punishments were likely to be the stocks, the pillory or a flogging. There were some criminals who had been sentenced to terms of imprisonment as a punishment, but they were in the minority.

However, apart from the common gaols there were other prisons called bridewells, or houses of correction. These were meant for vagrants, who were homeless people wandering about from place to place. In the house of correction they were supposed to work, learn industrious habits and be reformed from their idle ways. In fact it proved so difficult to find vagrants useful work that they were just locked up. This meant that in practice there was little to choose between the common gaol and the house of correction, save that debtors could only be sent to the former and vagrants to the latter.

Prison administration was chaotic. In theory all prisons belonged to the Crown: in practice they came under a variety of people. The county gaol was the responsibility of the sheriff but there were also town gaols, and there were even private gaols belonging to some of the bishops and nobility.

The Prison Governor was called the gaoler, and the warders were called turnkeys. They were very different from the professional prison officers we have today. The

Prisons in the eighteenth century

eighteenth century gaoler had no salary but instead had the right to make any money he could from his prisoners. There was a scale of fees — for admission, for discharge, for putting on irons, and for taking off irons. A prisoner who could not pay these fees had to stay in gaol even if the court had found him innocent or if he had finished his sentence. In addition, gaolers offered all sorts of comforts to the prisoners — at a price. Usually there was a tap-room that sold drink; it was possible to hire a bed, rather than sleep on the floor, or even to have a room to yourself. The gaoler would have any food you wanted brought in, provided you could pay his price.

From time to time the magistrates were supposed to visit the gaol in their area and see that it was in good order. But visiting prisons was so unpleasant that few magistrates would do this work, and usually the gaoler had everything his own way.

The larger prisons had some sort of plan. One part would be for debtors, and this had a masters' side and a common side. The masters' side was for those would could afford to pay for a room or a share in a room, while the common side was for those who could not. Common side debtors all lived together in considerable discomfort in one large room. Between the two would be a courtyard where the debtors could take exercise and play games during the day. Another part of the gaol was for criminals and here there would be one room for women and one for men. Again, there was a courtyard for exercise. There might even be a prison infirmary and a chapel, and a row of cells for those condemned to die.

Most prisons had not been built as such. The authorities converted parts of old castles or gateways. We hear of a room in a stable yard being used, and at Reading the gaol was three rooms in a public house. One disadvantage of this was that the prisons were not secure, especially as many of them were more or less in ruins. It would be expensive to repair them, so to stop their prisoners escaping gaolers loaded them with irons. One of the worst places for this was Ely, where the gaol belonged to the bishop. Each prisoner lay on his back wearing a spiked collar chained to the floor, and with a heavy bar over his legs. Floors were usually damp for there was no proper water supply and no sewers. Through fear of the prisoners escaping windows were as small as possible, so that ventilation was bad and the cells stank.

Today anyone in prison is fed at the public expense. In the eighteenth century the only public money available was 2d a day for each convicted criminal. This would buy him about one pound of bread. There was no allowance for any other prisoners, so that debtors and people, perhaps innocent, who were awaiting their trial had nothing. They relied on their families and friends to give them money to buy food from the gaoler. Those who had no one to help them were sometimes allowed to stand chained outside the prison gates and beg. At the Fleet Prison there was a special cell, with a grill opening on to the street, for this purpose.

From what has already been said, it is obvious that prisons were unhealthy places. Howard said that the typical criminal was young and robust: he would come to prison fit and healthy, but soon the foul building and the lack of food would take their toll, and if he lived to come out of prison it was probable that he could hardly walk and would take months to recover.

With prisoners crowded together, disease spread easily. The disease most dreaded was typhus, which was so common in prison that it was called 'gaol fever'. It is spread by lice which found a prison an ideal breeding ground. At Launceston in Cornwall, Howard found the prisoners in an offensive cell, where they stayed for days together, without coming out. He says:

> *Their provision was put down to them through a hole in the floor of the room above: and those who served them often caught the fatal fever. At my first visit I found the keeper, his assistant, and all the prisoners but one sick of it, and heard that but a few years before, many prisoners had died of it: and the keeper and his wife in one night.* (Ibid., p. 223.)

But prisons did more than endanger health. Most of them were small and the gaolers were unable and unwilling to classify their prisoners, so that children and adults, those waiting for trial, and those convicted, all lived together. The result was that the hardened criminals had every chance to be a bad influence on the others, particularly the children and young people. One man who felt strongly about this was the Rev John Clay, chaplain of Preston Gaol in the early nineteenth century. His son Walter Clay gives his father's views:

> *However bad a child may be previous to his entrance in Gaol, he generally feels a certain degree of terror associated with the idea of a prison, and consequently a hesitation in the commission of any crime which might lead to it. The prison once entered, however, the little culprit finds himself surrounded by those who make him ashamed, not for what he has done, but for the little that he has done. It is a melancholy truth that many young delinquents soon acquire an ambition to excel in crime.* (W. L. Clay, *The Prison Chaplain*, p. 13.)

When people in the nineteenth century became aware of what prisons were like, this was the problem that taxed them most. After all, it is not too difficult to build a prison that is clean and healthy, but how can we stop criminals from corrupting each other and instead turn them out into the world as reformed characters and decent citizens? This is a question which still has to be answered.

Prison reform

The first of the great prison reformers was John Howard (1726–90). He came to this work fairly late in life for it was not until he was made Sheriff of Bedfordshire at the age of forty-seven that he became interested in prisons. He was scandalised to see prisoners, found innocent at their trials, dragged back to gaol in irons because they could not pay their fees. He had a close look at Bedford Gaol and was horrified: he was determined to see if other prisons were as bad, and he found that they were. From then until he died he travelled throughout the British Isles and much of Europe, visiting prisons, and noting the sober but horrible facts that he discovered. The two extracts on page 103 are typical of his writing. In 1777 he published his book *The State of the Prisons* which distressed many who read it.

There have been few men more devoted and single-minded than Howard: no

Prison Reform

one could have been more careless of his own safety or more determined to help others in distress than he was. But he did have one weakness, and that was his rather reserved, morose temperament which stopped him co-operating with others. He did not inspire people to follow him, but instead worked alone.

None the less, once the need for prison reform had been so clearly shown there was no turning back. Around the country, men and women did what they could to reform their local prisons and from time to time Parliament passed Acts which made their work easier.

The first two Acts were introduced by an M.P. called Popham and became law in 1774. One was for preserving the health of prisoners, and ordered that the prisons should be cleaned, the prisoners washed, and that each prison should have a doctor to visit it. Since there was no machinery for enforcing this Act it was virtually in-effectual. Popham's second Act had more success and was an important reform: it said that prisoners found innocent at their trial must have their irons taken off at once and be set free in the open court.

After 1774 Parliament passed several more Acts, none of them very effective: then in 1823 it passed Peel's Gaol Act, which consolidated all the existing laws into one measure. This Act included many sound principles. Gaols were to be secure and healthy; some attempt had to be made to reform the prisoners: gaolers were to have salaries and not to charge fees, nor were they to sell things to prisoners; female prisoners were to have female warders; a chaplain and a surgeon were to visit the prisons regularly; gaolers could not put prisoners in irons without first telling the magistrates.

Unfortunately, this excellent Act had a fatal weakness: there was no way of making local authorities obey it. There should have been government inspectors to see that the law was carried out, but the Act did not provide for these and as a result many gaols remained as bad as they had ever been. Fortunately, however, there were in many areas people who were willing to take up the cause of prison reform.

One of these was a Gloucester magistrate, Sir George Paul. In 1786 Gloucester obtained a local Act of Parliament allowing it to build a new gaol at a cost of £50 000, and Paul was able to see that this prison was organised on sound prin-ciples. Prisoners were to have good food, clothing and bedding, there were to be no irons or chains, there were to be no fees, as the gaoler had a salary. But there was no attempt to make life easy for the prisoners. Each had his own cell and lived in solitary confinement, without seeing his friends. The only visitors he had were the warders and the governor, who came each day, and the chaplain and surgeon, who came each week. There was also hard labour which the regulations said should be 'of the hardest and most servile kind, in which drudgery is chiefly required, and where the work is little liable to be spoilt by ignorance, neglect, or obstinacy, such as treading in a wheel, or drawing in a capstan for turning a mill or other engines'.

Such was the model prison of Gloucester, which became a pattern for a good many others. While Paul and men like him concentrated on prison buildings and organisation, there were others who were determined to do what they could with the prisoners themselves. The most famous of these was Elizabeth Fry.

Mrs Fry was a Quaker and a woman of strong religious feelings. She was quiet and calm, but had a lot of character and was completely sure of herself. She was as single-minded and as determined as Howard but unlike Howard she could inspire and lead others. Her work started among the women prisoners at Newgate Gaol. She first visited this prison in 1813 and although she could do little at the time she was unable to forget what she had seen and made up her mind to return as soon as possible. In 1817 she formed a committee of ladies who called themselves the Association for the Improvement of Female Prisoners in Newgate. This Committee drew up a code of rules which the women prisoners promised to obey, brought in sewing materials, formed the women into working groups and then sold the goods that they made. They also organised schools, not only for the children but for the women also, since many of them were illiterate. The most important work of these schools was to teach religion – indeed, it was the central idea of Elizabeth Fry that to reform these women they must be given a firm religious faith. The idea worked. Soon the brawling and the fighting stopped, and the disorderly rabble of savage women began to behave decently. It was a great triumph and showed that religion, in the hands of the right person, could reform a criminal.

The work did not stop at Newgate since each year Mrs Fry went on a tour, visiting prisons, publishing what she found in them, addressing meetings and organising discussions. Wherever she went, Ladies' Prison Associations were organised and carried on her work in her absence.

During this time other people were also trying out their theories on how to reform criminals. They developed two systems that were important, and both came from America.

The first of these was the silent system, which aimed to stop prisoners corrupting each other by not allowing them to speak, and tried to reform them by making prison life so unpleasant that they would be too scared to come back. This was tried by Captain Elam Lynds, who became governor of Auburn Gaol in 1825. He instructed his warders to enforce absolute silence, and any prisoner who spoke was flogged with a cow-hide whip. The discipline in this prison was so savage that one convict cut off his own leg in protest.

In England two men who favoured the harsh treatment of prisoners were the Rev. Sydney Smith and Charles Dickens. Their idea was that criminals should do heavy, unpleasant labour. Sydney Smith wanted to see:

> Nothing but the treadwheel or the capstan, or some species of labour where the labourer could not see the result of his toil – where it is as monotonous, irksome and dull as possible. There should be no tea and sugar, no assemblage of female felons round the washing tubs – nothing but beating hemp, pulling oakum and pounding bricks. (S. and B. Webb, *English Prisons under Local Government*, p. 105.)

Many prisons followed these ideas. This is what it was like in Preston Gaol:

> The silent system is applied to a number of prisoners varying from forty to eighty. They are seated upon forms, are about nine feet apart, all facing the direction of the officer's raised desk, and all employed in picking cotton, except a few who are undergoing the punishment of compulsory idleness. At meals the same order is

observed. Throughout, the discipline is not merely that the silence of the tongue is observed — but the eye and the hand are mute. No sign, no look — whether of recognition to a fellow prisoner or of curiosity towards a visitor — is permitted, nor is it often attempted. A prisoner, recently committed, and not yet quite sober, once started up with an indignant exhortation, 'Britons never should be slaves'. A quiet smile on the face of some of the old gaol-birds was the only result: not a single head was turned while the recalcitrant Briton was removed from the room. (Clay, op. cit., p. 222.)

The prisoners described here had the light job of picking cotton, and suffered little more than boredom. There were alternative forms of work that were much more unpleasant. One was the treadwheel, which worked rather like the wheel in a mouse's cage, save that the prisoners stood at the top and at the outside. Convicts called it the 'everlasting staircase' but it was harder work than climbing stairs because the treads fell away beneath you as you stepped on them. The convicts toiled away for hours, always climbing upwards but never going anywhere.

Treadwheel and oakum shed, City Prison, Holloway. The treadwheel itself is hardly visible, but the men standing on the right are quite clearly climbing the 'everlasting staircase'. The men sitting down are picking oakum, that is unravelling lengths of old rope so that it could be made into doormats. It was a tedious and unpleasant job. Courtesy of Radio Times Hulton Picture Library.

Another machine was the crank. Working this was just like turning an old-fashioned mangle, and just about as hard. The prisoners had to turn the handle several thousand times a day if they wanted to be fed.

The alternative to the silent system was the separate system. Sir George Paul had used it at Gloucester and from there it had gone to America where they used it in the gaol at Philadelphia. Here they tried the experiment of seeing what would happen to convicts kept for long periods in solitary confinement and in complete darkness. Not surprisingly they went mad, and when the authorities tried the scheme in England they were a good deal less rigorous than they had been in Philadelphia. One of the first prisons to try out the system was Preston. Here they had a remarkable chaplain, the Rev John Clay, who was distressed at the brawling, the blasphemy and the swearing that went on while the prisoners were together in the yards. He would preach a sermon which seemed to influence the prisoners, but as soon as they had been back together in the yards for a few minutes it was obvious that all his good words had been forgotten. Eventually Clay persuaded the governor to try the separate system. Each prisoner was put in a cell on his own, where he had no contact at all with the others. Warders saw him every day, and the chaplain came to see him from time to time, but he spent long hours absolutely on his own. This is what Clay hoped would happen:

> In his cell he has no temptations from without: and many salutary admonitions from within. Active memory collects and brings before him anything that ever happened to him since he was a child: reflection traces painful results back to sinful causes: the sense of sin, and sorrow for it succeed: he is directed to Him who bore our sorrows and atoned for sin: then rises up a prayer for pardon, and he says 'By God's help I'll be a different man for the future.' (Ibid., p. 279.)

Whatever does go on in their minds, it is true that the strongest of men will break if they are in solitary confinement for long enough. Clay used to wait until his hardened criminal gave way and then he would do all he could to persuade him to lead a better life. Because he was a remarkable man he often succeeded, but the good work at Preston was probably due more to Clay's personality than to the system. Certainly Dickens thought poorly of the idea, and there is a scathing description of two 'converts' in *David Copperfield*. The Government, on the other hand, was convinced and separate confinement became official policy when Pentonville Prison was opened in 1842.

The separate system had one drawback. Too often the 'softening' process did not lead a man to repentance, but drove him instead to insanity and suicide. The model prison of Pentonville, clean, well planned, and well organised had a higher suicide rate than any of the older gaols.

Today all prisons are the property of the Crown and are the responsibility of the Home Secretary. It remains to see how this came about.

In the eighteenth century the government had already assumed responsibility for one type of convict – the man who had been sentenced to death but then had his punishment reduced to one of transportation. It was not too difficult to dispose of him: all that had to be done was to hand him over to a contractor who specialised in shipping criminals to the American colonies. Many Americans objected, among them Benjamin Franklin, who asked us if we would like to take their rattle snakes in exchange. This traffic came to an end in 1776 when the American War of Independence broke out. The Government had to act quickly, and converted old ships, known as hulks, into prisons. Not long afterwards the government found they could transport convicts to Australia, but the hulks remained as they were useful places to put those who were waiting for shipment.

In the early nineteenth century the government began to acquire prisons of

109

Prisons Act

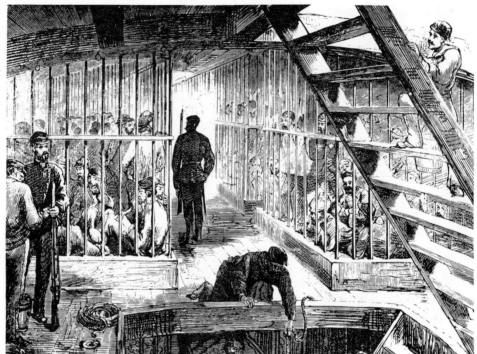

its own. In 1841 Millbank was opened, and in 1842 Pentonville. In 1850 Dartmoor, which had been used for French prisoners of war before 1815, was reopened as a state prison.

In 1852 the Australians refused to accept any more convicts. Even more prisons had to be opened and there had to be some system to replace transportation. To do so they introduced penal servitude. Under this, the convict first of all spent eighteen months under the separate system with its long periods of solitary confinement. Next he went on to work in some form of public works, for example, labouring in a naval dockyard. If he behaved himself, he would then have a 'ticket of leave', which meant he spent the last part of his sentence outside prison but with a few minor restrictions such as having to report to a police station from time to time.

Nor did the government neglect the older prisons. In 1835, it passed the first really effective Prisons Act. It was effective because it gave grants for the upkeep of prisons and appointed inspectors of prisons to see that the laws were obeyed. The final step came with the Prisons Act of 1877 which put all prisons under the direct control of the Home Secretary.

Probably the governments of the early nineteenth century showed more determination in tackling the problem of crime than they did any other social problem. By the 1850s the foundations of the modern police and prison services were well laid.

ORIGINAL SOURCES

Clay, W. L. *The Prison Chaplain*. 1861. An account of the separate system.
Colquhoun, Patrick. *Treatise on the Police of the Metropolis*. A lively account of crime in eighteenth century London.
Howard, John. *State of the Prisons*. Everyman's Library, Dent, London, 1929.
Mayhew, Henry and Binney, John. *The Criminal Prisons of London*, 1862. A full account of prison life.
Read, Charles. *It's Never too Late to Mend*, 1856. A description of the silent system at its worst.
The Third Report of the Committee on the Police of the Metropolis. Parliamentary Papers 1818 Vol. VIII. One of many Parliamentary Commissions on the police 1811–1835.

FURTHER READING

Brown, D. G. *The Rise of Scotland Yard*. Harrap, London, 1956.
Cobb, Belton. *The First Detectives*. Faber, London, 1957. This is easy to read and has many cases.
Collins, Philip. *Dickens and Crime*. Macmillan, London, 1962. This covers both police and prisons from an interesting angle.
Pringle, Patrick, ed. *Henry Goddard, Memoirs of a Bow Street Runner*, Museum Press, London, 1956.
Reith, Charles. *A New Study of Police History*. Oliver and Boyd, Edinburgh, 1956.
Ruggles-Brise, E. *The English Prison System*. Macmillan, London, 1921.
Webb. *English Prisons under Local Government*. English Local Government Vol. VI, Longman, London, 1922.

LITERARY SOURCES

Dickens, Charles. *David Copperfield*. Penguin, Harmondsworth, 1969. (Chapter 61: solitary confinement.)
Dickens, Charles. *Dombey and Son*. Penguin, Harmondsworth, 1970. (Chapters 33 and 34: return of a woman from transportation.)
Dickens, Charles. *Great Expectations*. Penguin, Harmondsworth, 1969. (Chapter 5: capture of two convicts escaping from the hulks; chapter 32: visit to Newgate; chapter 39: convict makes his fortune in Australia.)
Dickens, Charles. *Oliver Twist*. Penguin, Harmondsworth, 1970. (Chapter 22: a burglary; chapter 31: Bow Street Runners.)
Dickens, Charles. *Pickwick Papers*. Macmillan, London, 1968. (Chapter 6: return from transportation.)
Dickens, Charles. *Reprinted Papers*. Everyman's Library, Dent, London, 1970. The Detective Police; Down with the Tide (river police).
Dickens, Charles. *Sketches by Boz*. Everyman's Library, Dent, London, 1968. (Scenes, chapter 25: visit to Newgate; Characters, chapter 12: prisoners' van.)
Dickens, Charles. *The Uncommercial Traveller*. Everyman's Library, Dent, London, 1969. (Chapter 5: tour around Liverpool with the police; chapter 30: criminals.)

10 Education

IN 1841 A VISITOR TO WOLVERHAMPTON CALLED HORNE SPOKE WITH AN EIGHTEEN-year-old factory girl. This is how he described her education:

> *Can read in the Bible and Prayer Book: reads other books when she can get them: can't write at all, not her own name. Was at a day-school six years: left when she was ten years old. Never plays at any games: when she goes home after her work she reads for her father and mother: they are old: never heard of St. Valentine's day: does not know what a country dance is: was never at a dance in her life: never saw a dance: never heard of Harlequin and Columbine: has no idea what they are like. Does not know what month it is, nor what year: what she thinks most of when she is alone is her books. She would like very much to go to school: she feels she has a great deal to learn. (Parliamentary Papers, 1842, Vol. XV, Evidence 31.)*

This girl was above the average. She had been to school longer than most, she was interested in learning and in books, and from the way she answered other questions about her work she was obviously quite intelligent. Yet she could not write, she was ignorant of the most elementary things, and she was leading a life that was drab and uninteresting in the extreme. There were many worse than her. Horne went on to speak with more children and young people and this is what he concluded:

> *The state of ignorance of things in general is conspicuous. Many who have attended Sunday schools for three or four years can neither read nor write. You will find boys who have never heard of such a place as London, nor of Willenhall (which is only three miles distant), who have never heard the name of the Queen — or who have believed that Her Majesty's name was Prince Albert. You will find poor girls who have never sung or danced: never seen a dance: never read a book that made them laugh: never seen a violet, or a primrose: and others whose only idea of a green field was derived from having been stung by a nettle. (Ibid., q. 19.)*

This was bad enough, but what the Victorians found even more shocking was ignorance about God and religion. When the Vicar of Sedgely asked a miner if he knew Jesus Christ the man replied, 'Does 'a work down the pit?' These are the answers given by a boy coal-miner to questions on religion:

I never went to a day school or Sunday-school. I got no clothes to go in: I cannot read or write: I never heard of Jesus Christ. I don't know what you mean by God. I never heard of Adam or know what you mean by Scripture: I have heard of a Bible, but don't know what 'tis all about: I don't know what will become of me hereafter if I am wicked. I have never been told: I don't know what Sunday is: there are six days in the week: I remember now that there is another day: father gets tipsy at Betty Bilsen's sometimes. (Parliamentary Papers, 1842, Vol. XII, p. 121.)

Many of the reasons for this ignorance are obvious from the other chapters of this book. Too many towns were a wasteland of slums with no parks, museums, art galleries or libraries. All they had to offer the working man was the public house and the occasional tawdry theatre. Hours of work were so long that people had little time or energy to do anything intelligent, even if the opportunities had been there. Children started work so young that few of them had the chance to go to school for a reasonable number of years. On top of all this, such schools as there were were inadequate and inefficient.

Charity schools

These were the oldest and were organised by the Society for the Promotion of Christian Knowledge which was founded in 1699. One of its main aims was to encourage people to build schools for poor children and many such schools had sprung up all over the country. Sometimes a rich man would pay for a school, but more often a group of people would join together to make donations for the building and then give subscriptions each year to pay for the running expenses. The children usually had a uniform and the school was known by its colour. Northampton had a Blue Coat School, a Brown Coat School, an Orange Coat School and a Green Coat School.

These schools tried to do a lot for their children. The classroom work was simple enough – religion, reading, writing and arithmetic – but the pupils also learnt practical things that would help them in later life. Girls learnt to knit, sew and cook, while boys learned all manner of crafts, such as weaving, gardening and even ploughing. The schools helped the children to find good jobs when they left. They also gave them free school uniforms, although this was not such a popular idea with the children. Not only did the uniform show the school quite clearly, but there was a metal plate with a number attached to it. Any member of the public who saw a child misbehaving could report him by taking his number.

It was not easy to find a place in a Charity School. This is part of the will of Gabriel Newton who left money for the Green Coat School, Northampton. He said his money was to be used for:

Clothing, schooling and educating 25 boys of indigent and necessitous parents of the Established Church of England. Each boy to be allowed annually a green cloth coat, waistcoat and breeches, not under 20d a yard, one shirt of flaxen cloth, not under 13d a yard, with stockings, cap etc: and the residue yearly paid to teach the boys reading, writing and arithmetic and singing of psalms and toning the responses in divine service in the parish church. No boy to be admitted if the parents received relief from the parish. (History of the Town of Northampton, pp. 36—7.)

Thus, the parents had to fulfil three conditions. They had to be members of the Church of England, they had to be poor, but they had to manage without poor relief. Even this was not enough. The boy or girl had to be nominated by one of the wealthy people who subscribed to the school. As most schools took only twenty or thirty pupils, nominations were few.

The Charity Schools did good work, but they helped only a minority of the population.

Sunday Schools

These were the first schools to try to help the mass of the population. How or where they began is not at all clear, but a man who did important work in the late eighteenth century was Robert Raikes of Gloucester.

In Gloucester there was a pin factory where children worked hard for six days a week. On Sunday, their one free day, they roamed the streets in gangs and Raikes was horrified at their bad language and the damage they did. He decided to open a Sunday School for them, to teach them to read the Bible, and so, he hoped, encourage them to have better habits. Soon people all over the country were following Raikes's example.

But the Sunday Schools laboured under considerable difficulties. Few of them had suitable buildings: they were often overcrowded and teachers and pupils alike had the poor man's dread of fresh air. The atmosphere in these schools quickly became foul and it was quite usual for the pupils to be carried out fainting. There was no way to compel children to go to Sunday School – attendance depended on persuasion from the teachers and parents. Not unnaturally, children who had been cooped up in factories or workshops all the week were not keen to spend much of Sunday in a reeking classroom.

Teachers were unqualified and unpaid. This is what was said of the Sunday School teachers of Willenhall:

> *Not any of them have been trained as teachers, nor have any of them received other education than such as they communicate in these schools, consequently some of them cannot write — not even their own names.*
>
> *The superintendent teachers are locksmiths, key-makers, miners and other manufacturers and tradesmen of the place, either small masters or journeymen: and the Sunday school at Short Heath is superintended by a very worthy and honest-minded butty of a coal-mine. (Parliamentary Papers, 1842, Vol. XV, q. 51.)*

Sunday Schools did not attempt to teach a great deal. Obviously religion was important for them, and so that they could use their Bibles and Prayer Books, the children had to learn to read. Usually the schools did not teach writing, partly because some people thought it was not proper to write on a Sunday, and partly because many of the teachers could not write themselves. The Wolverhampton schools were typical:

RULES

TO BE OBSERVED BY PARENTS AND OTHERS,

ON THE ADMISSION OF THEIR CHILDREN INTO THE

PAROCHIAL GIRLS' SCHOOL

BELONGING TO THE

PARISH OF ST. SEPULCHRE, LONDON.

THE Children are to be at School every Morning at Nine o'Clock, Sundays excepted; they will leave School at Twelve o'Clock; they are to return to School at Two o'Clock, except on Wednesdays and Saturdays, which are half-holidays, and remain there till Four o'Clock, from Michaelmas to Lady-Day, and from Lady-Day to Michaelmas till half-past Four o'Clock. On Sundays they are to be at the School at a quarter past Ten in the Morning, and at half-past Six in the Evening. No other holidays allowed, except a fortnight at Christmas, three weeks at Midsummer, and a week at Easter.

The Parents or Friends are to see that their Children **leave home in proper time,** that they may be in their places at School by Nine and Two o'clock; they are to send them **well washed and combed,** with their Hair cut short, and their Clothes well mended; they will not be allowed to wear Earrings, or any other ornaments.

If from Sickness or any other reasonable cause a Child cannot attend, **immediate notice** must be given to the Mistress; if this be omitted, or if the Girl's absence be not properly accounted for, the Parents must attend the next meeting of the Committee.

When it is intended to withdraw a Child from the School, one of the Parents or Friends must attend the Committee, to signify such intention.

The Childrens' best Clothes are to remain in the School during the week, in a bag provided for that purpose; they are to be given to the Girls on Saturday, and to be returned in perfect order on the Monday after.

On leaving the School from day to day, the Children are to **return quietly home.**

In any communications that may pass between the Parents or Friends of the Children and the Mistress, they are to behave with civility and respect; when required by the Mistress, they are to attend the Committee, with their Children, to answer any complaint that may be brought against them.

The Children will be entirely under the control of the Mistress and the Committee, one of whom visits the School every week; their Parents must therefore freely submit them to reproof and correction, and should there be any just cause of complaint. the same must be made to the Committee at their next Meeting.

G. ROSS, Printer, 3, King Street, Snow Hill, E.C.

Rules of a Charity School.
Clearly the girls are to behave like young ladies and they and their parents must agree with strict discipline in the school. Many parents wanted a place for their child in a Charity School. as this meant they had the best education a working class child could hope to find. The schools could pick and choose their pupils and enforce strict rules on dress and behaviour.
Courtesy of Guildhall Library, City of London.

Private schools

> *Religion and moral instruction is all they really profess to communicate, and this is very seriously and assiduously attempted by teaching the children to read religious books. The children learn to read these in a loud monotonous, sing-song voice, with no attention to punctuation, and with no sort of comprehension of the meaning of what they read.*
>
> *Of the singing of the children at Sunday Schools, it must be pronounced intolerable.* (Op. cit., q. 17.)

Even in their main subjects of religion and reading few pupils made much progress. They could attend Sunday School for years without learning to read, and could leave imagining, for example, that Goliath was one of the Apostles.

But the Sunday Schools played their part, none the less. They were the first schools to attempt to bring some sort of education to the mass of the people and they were the first schools to open their doors to any child who wished to attend. Their very failure was important, for it showed that if the children of the poor were to have a proper education, then they would have to come to school through the week.

Private schools

Private schools for children of the poor were usually little more than baby-minding establishments. Mothers who went to work paid a small fee so that their children would be under the eyes of an adult. Most of the teachers in charge of these schools knew nothing about teaching and the school rooms themselves were usually overcrowded and insanitary. This is an account of a private school in Liverpool.

> *Mr Wood found a school in a garret up three flights of dark, broken stairs, with 40 children in the compass of 10 feet by 9 and where, on a perch, sat a cock and two hens. Under a stump bed immediately beneath was a dog kennel, in the occupation of three black terriers, whose barking, added to the noise of the children and the cackling of the fowls, was almost deafening. There was only one small window, at which sat the master, obstructing three fourths of the light which it was capable of admitting.* (State of the Towns Commission, App: Pt II, p. 30.)

Few of these private schools did work that was of any value at all.

Monitorial schools

In the early nineteenth century two men gave a lot of thought to the problem of providing full-time education to the children of the poor. They were Joseph Lancaster and Andrew Bell. Lancaster was a Quaker while Bell was an Anglican clergyman, so that while their ideas on education were much the same, they disagreed over religion and were soon bitter rivals. Nonconformists tended to follow Lancaster, while members of the Church of England followed Bell.

Lancaster made the first important move in 1803 when he wrote his book *Improvements in Education*, and in 1808 his supporters formed the Royal Lancasterian

Society to advance his ideas. They shortly afterwards changed their name to the British and Foreign Schools Society, as Lancaster had proved so difficult that they had expelled him. Schools connected with this society called themselves British Schools for short.

In 1811 Bell and his friends in the Church of England founded the National society for Promoting the Education of the Poor in the Principles of the Established Church. Their rivals called these schools Bellian Schools, but members of the society, not surprisingly, preferred to call them National Schools.

In spite of the competition between the two societies, both organised their schools on much the same lines. They had, after all, the same problems: a chronic shortage of money and trained teachers. Each school was to have only one adult teacher, but both Lancaster and Bell claimed that the teacher was able to control a school of several hundred children. This he did with the help of monitors. The monitors were the older and brighter children and they had to come to school early to have their lessons before the others arrived. Through the day each monitor took a small group of children and taught them what he had learned himself in the morning. This was very like the factory system brought to school, for instead of minding

A monitorial school, Clapham. This was a National School organised on Bell's plan. It is easy to pick out the small groups of pupils, each in the charge of its monitors. The youngest children are learning to write on a sand table.
Courtesy of Greater London Council.

AN INTERNAL VIEW OF CLAPHAM SCHOOL.
Conducted on the System of the *MADRAS SCHOOL Invented by Andrew Bell D.D. &c.*
This School was erected in 1810 for the Education of 200 Boys.

117

machines the young workers minded small groups of children. The master or mistress was like the foreman, who only needed to step in when something serious went wrong.

These ideas had instant appeal. Many people had felt the need to provide schools for the poor, but had not seen how it could be done. Now Bell and Lancaster seemed to have found the answer and many new schools were founded. In the towns and villages the wealthier people made donations for the building of a school, and also agreed to subscribe a certain amount of money each year to help pay the running expenses. These subscribers met annually and elected a group of managers, who were responsible for the day to day running of the school, the care of the building and the keeping of the accounts. Almost always the man to start this was the local clergyman who had to do most of the work himself.

Subscriptions did not meet all the expenses of running the school. Poor parents themselves were expected to pay a few pence each week in school fees. As time went on, subscriptions from the rich dwindled but school fees went up, so that by 1870 in an average school they provided about one-third of its income. This was particularly true of the British Schools, whose managers found they could attract the children of wealthier parents – skilled workers and shopkeepers – by charging higher fees. The Church of England remained faithful to the idea of helping the very poor so the National Schools kept their fees much lower, and often allowed children to attend for nothing.

The buildings of these monitorial schools were simple. There was usually just one large school room with no separate classrooms, for the teacher could not trust his monitors to take their groups on their own: he had to keep the entire school under his eye. Then, as now, land was expensive in towns so it was rare for schools to have attractive sites or playgrounds. This is a description of the schools of Nottingham in 1844:

> *The school rooms are, with few exceptions, bad as regards site, light, height and ventilation. Warmth is in most cases afforded by open fireplaces, and is not distributed with sufficient equality. I do not bear in mind any public school with a playground attached.*
>
> *St Mary's School (recently erected) is, from want of available land, built in the corner of a crowded burial ground, immediately fronting another similar place of interment, and alongside an alley in the occupation of the lowest characters. The British Boys' and Girls' School is built on a public sewer, and the structure is at present sinking in consequence. The Boys' National School is in one of the most vicious and degraded neighbourhoods. To these important schools the public street is the only playground.* (Ibid., p. 133.)

The monitorial schools did not teach many subjects. As in the Sunday Schools, it was religion that mattered most, since the people who put up the money hoped, above everything, for a reform of the morals of the working classes. In the National Schools the vicar or the curate often made a point of doing this important teaching himself. After religion it was reading that mattered most, since the children could not use their Bibles and Prayer Books until they were able to read. As they could not afford books, the teachers used to hang reading sheets on the walls of the schoolroom and the children used to stand round them in their little groups. Incidentally, in those days pupils did not put their hands up – they put them forward. This is easier to do, causes less inconvenience to the next child, and in a small group of six or eight is just as easy to see.

Unlike the Sunday Schools the monitorial schools also taught writing – usually on slates – and arithmetic. Girls might also learn plain needlework and knitting.

Attendance at these schools was a problem, as it was with the Sunday Schools. We have seen that they charged fees, which put off enough parents: but it was not really finding the twopence or threepence a week that bothered most of them. The main difficulty was that a child at school was not earning money. As a result, the parents usually sent their children to school when they were young, but as soon as they could go to work, often at eight or nine years old, they took them away. Attendance at school was usually best among country girls, because there was little enough work for many of them to do on the farms until they were twelve or over.

In spite of all their difficulties these schools could succeed with a few of their pupils. These are the answers William Carter of Wolverhampton gave to questions on mental arithmetic and religious knowledge. He was fifteen years old and had been at the National School at Wolverhampton for seven years.

> *1,000 lbs of beef at 6d per lb would come to £25: 115½ lbs of beef at 6d per lb would come to £2.17.3d. 5 cwts of soap at 4d per lb would come to £9.6.8d. The interest of £4,000 for 9 months at 5% is £150: the discount off £320.9.2d at 10% would be £32.011d. For £50 worth of locks at 75% discount he would have to receive £13.10s – no – £12.10s.*
>
> *The Red Sea was in Arabia, to the West, between Arabia and Egypt: the head of John the Baptist was cut off to please Herodias, she having pleased Herod by dancing before him.* (Parliamentary Papers, 1842. Vol. XV, Evidence 109, q. 24.)

But William Carter was quite exceptional. Few children who came to the monitorial schools up to the age of eight or nine could have learnt much. The evidence given by the factory children to various Royal Commissions is depressing proof of this. Yet the monitorial schools played a vital part in the history of education in this country. Private schools for the poor, Charity Schools and Sunday Schools were all incapable of much useful development. But when monitorial schools had help and guidance from the state they grew into efficient schools, and this started to happen in the second half of the century. The much-needed help and guidance was already on its way before 1850.

Government interest in education began with the factory children. Enlightened employers like Robert Owen had already been providing schools for their child workers but such schools were voluntary in two senses: the children only attended if they wished to do so, and the employer was not bound to provide the school. Most employers were unwilling to build schools and most parents were unwilling to make their children attend, so the government decided to try compulsion.

The first Act of Parliament to be at all effective was Althorp's Factories Regulation Act of 1833. This limited the hours a child could work and also said that he could

Ragged schools

not come to the factory unless he brought with him a certificate to say that he had attended school for at least twelve hours during the previous week. One of the duties of the Factory Inspector was to see that this was done. A later Act in 1844 reduced the hours in the factory still further, and would not allow a child to work more than half a day. He then had to spend the other half day in school, attending for at least three hours.

These two Acts had very limited results. In the first place they applied only to children in textile mills, who were a tiny minority of the child population and even with these children there was little success. Attending school did not necessarily mean having a good education. This is an account of a school attended by factory children:

> The children were playing in the open yard, and the master was engaged in sawing up the blackboard. The children were summoned into the schoolroom: they entered disorderly and careless. In the meantime two girls, lying upon the top of the inner porch of the door, and amusing themselves with their playmates, were ordered down to join the others. The master then drew from his pocket a whistle, and blew the signal for attention: he then produced his books and materials for teaching, which consisted of six dilapidated Bibles, some copy books, one slate, half a dozen loose and ragged leaves of Reading Made Easy and the remains of the blackboard. The pretence of discipline and system in the exhibition of his pocket-whistle — the only whole and unbroken implement of his calling — contrasted with the deplorable aspect of his room, the miserable remnants of his books, and the surviving fragments of the blackboard, supported on either side by a hand-saw and a hammer, was in itself intensely ludicrous: but the injury this man was inflicting upon his scholars by the daily repetition of this farce of teaching, might be incalculable. (Parliamentary Papers, 1854, Vol. XIX, p. 306.)

Committee of Council for Education

The attempt to force an education on the factory children was largely a failure because neither employers, parents, nor children would co-operate. The government had more success when, instead of attempting to coerce the unwilling, it gave help to those who were trying to help themselves.

This first happened in 1833 when Parliament decided to make a grant of £20 000 to help pay for new school buildings. The money was made over to the National Society and the British and Foreign School Society, with one important condition attached. Local subscriptions had to pay at least half the cost of a new building; if this happened, then government money could be used to pay the remainder. £20 000 was not a lot for the whole country, but what was important was the idea behind the grant. Where local people were willing to make a determined effort the state would now encourage them. This was the beginning of the partnership between central and local authorities which has decided, and still does decide, the shape of English education. Parliament renewed the grant for education every year and from time to time increased it. By 1846 it had grown to £100 000 and by 1859 it was over £800 000.

Another important development was the organisation of a government department to look after education. Obviously Parliament was not going to grant money year after year without appointing someone to see that it was spent in the proper way. Accordingly, in 1839 a committee of the Privy Council was set up to do this work. It had the official title of The Committee of Council for Education and was the forerunner of the Ministry of Education which we have today.

Fortunately, the Secretary of the Committee of Council was a remarkable man. He was Dr Kay, who has been mentioned elsewhere in this book, though by now he had changed his name to Kay Shuttleworth. In his earlier career as a doctor he had worked among the poor of Manchester and had seen their suffering. Most of their misery, he felt, they could cure for themselves but they were unable to do so because of their ignorance. He became convinced that it was only through education that the lot of the poor could be improved so he was more than pleased to take the post of Secretary to the Committee of Council for Education.

At this time most of the schools were monitorial schools, based on the systems of Bell and Lancaster. Kay Shuttleworth knew full well that such schools might instruct children in elementary reading, writing and arithmetic, but their instruction was purely mechanical: it would never produce educated people. Only good teachers can give a good education and these were in short supply. How was Kay Shuttleworth to find all the teachers the schools would need?

Part of the answer was to have colleges for training teachers. There had been a plan for a state college but as it had come to nothing, Kay Shuttleworth and his friend E. C. Tufnell set up their own at Battersea as a private venture. This was in 1839 and by 1842 the Government had been persuaded to make a grant of £1000 to the college. Fortunately the British and Foreign Schools Society and the National Society also realised the need for colleges and built their own. The National Society was especially active so that by 1845 it had twenty-two colleges.

But where were the new colleges to find their recruits? Kay Shuttleworth discovered the answer during a visit to Holland, where he saw young people serving as teacher apprentices in the schools. This was an idea borrowed from industry.

Pupil teachers

A boy or girl aged about fourteen would be apprenticed to a master and in the same way that the apprentice craftsman did simple jobs in the workshop, the apprentice teacher did simple jobs in the classroom. As his skill increased, so he did more complicated work until finally he qualified as a master himself.

Kay Shuttleworth was so impressed by what he saw in Holland that in 1846 he persuaded the Committee of Council to accept a scheme for the training of pupil teachers. These young people were still pupils; they had to carry on their own studies, taking such subjects as English, mathematics, history, geography and science. It was the duty of their headmaster to give them seven and a half hours teaching every week, which he had to do either before or after school. But the apprentice was also a teacher and he had to work for five and a half hours each day in the classroom. At the end of each year the pupil teacher had to sit an examination and at the end of his fifth year he took what was known as the Queen's Scholarship Examination. If he passed this he was given a government grant so that he could go to a training college. To encourage young people to become pupil teachers the government paid them a small wage, and to encourage schools to employ them the government paid them a grant, which was usually added to the headmaster's salary.

It was not an easy life for a pupil teacher. This is how a Bath clergyman described it:

> After a hard day's work in school, the schoolmaster has to set to work to prepare his teachers: perhaps he has three or four all in different years, all requiring a certain amount of help, to whom he was pledged to give seven and a half hours instruction per week, by the terms of his agreement. In order to accomplish this, the teachers must either break into the few precious hours of rest allowed them in the evening, or, as I believe is commonly the practice, take the pupil teachers immediately after school when both are jaded by a long day of wearisome work in an atmosphere not too pure. And what have they to work at? Dry elementary subjects, important to learn, but very dull to grind at year after year, on top of an equally dull grind at still more dry and still more elementary work in the day school: and remember that these subjects have to be most carefully taught, not got through, not shirked, but beaten inch by inch, a scrap of grammar, a scrap of geography, a scrap of history, a scrap of Euclid, and all to be taught in a high and dry way. (Bath Chronicle, 17 February 1876.)

Some pupil teachers found their studies too much for them. One headmistress wrote:

> On Tuesday I gave Amy Hallows the following question: 'Give some account of the conversion of this country to Christianity.' She said 'Pope Gregory sent St. Augustine and 40 monks here to convert the people, afterwards Pope Gregory came over and married Bertha of France and she converted him.' I was much disappointed by this thoughtless and foolish answer. (Log Book, Weymouth House School, Bath.)

Not many pupil teachers were a lot of use in the classroom, particularly in the early years of their apprenticeship. A head complained:

> *Oral lesson by P. T. Hudson on 'the apple'. The lesson was too advanced for the lower classes and not given in the way that would interest any class. He failed to train out a single point and eventually lost control of the children.* (Ibid.)

Quite large numbers of pupil teachers gave up the struggle and left to take other jobs, but some fought their way through. They passed their Queen's Scholarship Examination, went to college and returned to the schools, to train more pupil teachers themselves. It was a hard way to learn a profession, in many respects it was a bad way, but in nineteenth century England it was probably the only way. Kay Shuttleworth's system produced a race of teachers that were none too well educated, were narrow and too harsh; but they were a hardy race which they needed to be to educate and discipline the children of those days.

How much progress was made in education? In 1858 the government appointed a Royal Commission to investigate. The Duke of Newcastle was chairman so it is known as the Newcastle Commission.

The Newcastle Commission reported in 1861 and found a lot to criticise. Most children who went to school left early – barely a fifth stayed over the age of eleven, and very few over the age of twelve. During their years at school their attendance was usually bad. Teaching methods, though improved since the days of monitorial schools, were still too mechanical and the curriculum of the schools rarely went beyond the three Rs and religion. On the other hand there had been progress. In 1800 only one child in thirty-one was at school and large numbers had never attended at all. But by 1860 most children attended school for at least a year or two, while the proportion actually in school at any one time had risen to one in eight. This still seems small compared with today when every child is at school, but we must remember the rapid growth in the population that took place between 1800 and 1860. The school population had not only kept pace – it had grown over two and a half times as quickly. This was a tribute, partly, to the help given by the government, but it was mainly due to voluntary efforts. The people who mattered most were the clergy. In the towns and villages they had organised public opinion, raised money, built schools and then supervised them. No clergyman was happy if his parish was without a school, and he would do all he could to provide one. Church of England clergy disagreed with Nonconformists and Roman Catholics about religious teaching in the schools, and in some ways this hampered the growth of education – but Parliament and governments were slow in coming to the idea that it was the duty of the state to provide education, so it was fortunate that in the meantime there were plenty of volunteers to undertake the work.

No less important than the supply of buildings was the supply of teachers and we have seen how Kay Shuttleworth's scheme of training pupil teachers was beginning to answer this need. In 1860 much remained to be done, but the idea of elementary education for all was now in sight, and by 1870 W. E. Forster was able to persuade Parliament to pass an Education Act that aimed to provide a school place for every child in the country.

Education

ORIGINAL SOURCES

Bernard, Sir Thomas. *Of the Education of the Poor*, 1809.
Brougham, Henry. *Observations on the Education of the People*. 1825.
Lancaster, Joseph. *Improvements in Education*. 1803.
Royal Commission on Elementary Education. (The Newcastle Commission's report on elementary education.) Parliamentary Papers Vol XXI, 1861.
Trimmer, Sarah. *Reflections on the Education of Children in Charity School*. 1792.

FURTHER READING

Adamson, J. W. *English Education 1789–1902*. C.U.P., Cambridge, 1965.
Jones, M. J. *The Charity School Movement*. Cass, London, 1963.
Sutherland, Gillian. *Elementary Education in the Nineteenth Century*. Historical Association, London, 1971.

LITERARY SOURCES

Dickens, Charles. *Nicholas Nickleby*. Blackie, Glasgow, 1962. (Chapter 8: Dotheboys Hall.
Dickens, Charles. *Our Mutual Friend*. Penguin, Harmondsworth, 1971. (Book 2, Chapter 1: the elementary school.)
Dickens, Charles. *Sketches by Boz*. Everyman's Library, Dent, London, 1968. (Our parish: Chapter 6: Charity School children.)
Dickens, Charles. *The Uncommercial Traveller*. Everyman's Library, Dent, London, 1969. (Chapter 12: the Mechanics' Institute; Chapter 21: a pauper school.)

Irish immigration 11

THE PROBLEMS OF IMMIGRATION ARE NOT NEW TO TWENTIETH CENTURY BRITAIN. THE large numbers of desperately poor and mostly unskilled Irish immigrants to nineteenth century Britain created problems which were just as serious as those of today, if not more so.

The Irish have been coming to Britain for centuries: the shortness of the crossing and the cheapness of the passage have made immigration easy. From early in the eighteenth century there was a seasonal invasion of harvesters who came over for the summer to work on English or Scottish farms. In 1841, for instance, the number of seasonal workers entering Britain was 57 651, some of whom paid as little as 6d a head for their passage. But the early nineteenth century saw an increase also in the number of permanent immigrants who came to this country to settle. By the mid-1830s the annual figure of Irish immigrants to England and Wales had reached 250 000. In the normal course of events these figures would have increased slowly but steadily over the next few decades, but in fact the course of events was not normal. The series of potato famines culminating in the disastrous Great Famine of 1845–1848 caused a sudden and massive increase in the immigration figures. Between 1841 and 1861 the number of Irish-born in England was more than doubled. To take one town alone – Birmingham – the figure of 4683 Irish in 1841 rose to 11 332 in 1861, approximately 6 per cent of the borough's population.

Up to 1845 the population of Ireland had grown steadily, but there had been no growth of industry to provide the extra jobs needed. Fear of possible competition had led the British Government to discourage Irish industry and in any case Ireland lacked the two essentials for industrial expansion – iron and coal. There had been a certain amount of cotton and woollen manufacture but these collapsed in the face of competition from Lancashire and Yorkshire.

Only in Ulster was there anything like a prosperous industry, based on the manufacture of linen. Ireland was a land of peasant farmers, scraping a living from the soil. Agricultural methods remained primitive because there were few enlightened landlords to encourage the new methods that had achieved success in England. Particularly in the west and south of the country, farms were divided again and again as each generation grew up, until it was quite usual for a family to exist on the produce of one acre or less. In our climate, there is only one crop which will give sufficient food from such a small patch of land, and that is the potato; consequently the poorer Irish families grew potatoes and nothing else. When the potato crop was lost through blight, as it was in 1845, 1846 and 1848, the result was starvation and disease on a terrible scale.

Irish immigration

A Connemara cabin. Connemara is in the far west of Ireland. It was one of the most backward areas, and one that was badly hit by the potato famine. Emigrants coming from conditions like these found it difficult to adjust to life in a large city in England.
Courtesy of *Illustrated London News.*

The conditions of life of the Irish peasantry were extremely primitive. The Irish Census of 1841 reported that three-fifths of the population of the western part of the country were living in what were described as fourth class habitations – windowless single-roomed mud cabins with little or no furniture. It was from areas such as this that most of the Irish immigrants to England came. They were ill-prepared for city life, and in their desperation were ready to take any job, however menial, and to put up with any lodging, however squalid. They made for those places in England which could afford to give poor relief – the large towns, the three chief areas of settlement being Lancashire, Glasgow and London. The local authorities in England were already overburdened, as we have seen, with their own poor, and the arrival of large numbers of 'pauper Irish' caused resentments and tensions. Thus the Irish became scapegoats: many of the social problems we have described in earlier chapters of this book were laid at their door. There were demands for a control on the number of Irish immigrants entering the country. In April 1849, for instance, under the heading 'The Irish Plague', the *Cardiff and Merthyr Guardian* protested that 'Upwards of 50 Irish wretches, in a most deplorable plight, were landed on Penarth beach and proceeded on to Cardiff. Some check must be put to the thousands of Irish paupers who flock into the country.'

The Emigrants,
by Erskine Nicol.
This is a typical
piece of Victorian
sentimentality, but it
does show the deep
and complex
emotions that
emigrating involved.
These two are not
running from the
famine; indeed the
picture was painted
some sixteen years
later. But after the
famine, emigration
was common.
Ireland could ill
afford to lose its
young people, but
there was nothing
for them at home, so
they left in their
tens of thousands.
Courtesy of the
Tate Gallery,
London.

Life in England

Probably the immigrants found that life in England was easier than in Ireland, but it was still harsh enough. Most of the men were unskilled and used to hard physical labour on the land, so the work they were given was nearly always rough and they had to take jobs that the English would not do themselves. A Liverpool builder gave these figures to show the occupations of the 7500 Irish workers in the town in 1835:

Mechanics of various sorts	780
Brickworkers	270
Sugar boilers	200
Masons' labourers	350
Bricklayers' labourers	850
Chemical works and soaperies	600
Sawyers	80
Labourers in smithies, lime kilns, plasterers' yards and paviors	340
Lumpers about the docks	1700
Porters employed in warehousing goods	1900
Coal heavers and sundry	430
	7500

(*Report on the State of the Irish Poor in England*, 1835, p. 29.)

This list is not accurate, but it gives a fair impression of the kind of work done by the Irish. The only skilled men here are the 'mechanics of various sorts' who make up just over one tenth of the total. The largest two groups by far are the lumpers in the docks and the porters in the warehouses, where the work was hard, dangerous and insecure.

Early in the nineteenth century the Irish became an important force in the building industry. Then as now they specialised in heavy construction work, moving around the country from site to site as the network of canals, docks and, later, railways expanded to meet the great industrial boom. Besides the ordinary labourers who did the digging and shovelling there were the 'navvies', originally the 'navigators' who learnt their trade in the construction of waterways but who later found work in the making of railways and roads, who did the difficult and dangerous jobs like tunnelling. Working in gangs of twelve, these men were famous for their endurance, their loyalty to each other and their fearlessness. It must always be remembered that there were no mechanical drills or bulldozers to take the place of back-breaking toil: every inch of tunnel or embankment was the result of human muscle-power. Like their twentieth century successors who worked on the motorways and power stations of modern Britain, the Irish were popular with contractors because of their mobility and lack of family ties: they lived in temporary camps near the site, often far from cities, remaining separate from the local community.

The expanding cotton spinning and weaving industries of the north-west were another important source of more stable employment for the Irish, and often whole families, including the women and children, were engaged in this work. Those who had worked in the Irish linen mills were already experienced handloom weavers and found it easy to get work in the cotton mills of Lancashire and Scotland. But industry was not the only source of employment. Single women were in demand as domestic servants, while many of the men enlisted in the ranks of armed services. An English gentleman writer in 1835 noted the high proportion of Irish in the armed services at that time, remarking grandly that 'Irishmen may freely man our navy, or serve in our armies, because we do not desire that employment for ourselves. It is more problematical whether they may officer them, because that is more genteel and lucrative, and should therefore be reserved for ourselves.' (*Westminster Review*, January 1835, p. 86.)

On the whole, the Irish were content to remain in labouring jobs and were rather despised by the English for their lack of ambition. Some found their way into the lower middle-class as shopkeepers, pawnbrokers, publicans and tradesmen, mainly serving the needs of their own community, but unlike the Jews, they lacked the education, initiative and urban tradition to achieve wider financial success. Some young Irishmen achieved celebrity through their skill with their fists, and pugilism offered a quick road to money and fame for a few.

Wages

As the Irish did the worst jobs, generally speaking they earned the lowest wages. At home they had been used to living at subsistence level and so even the lowest English wages were an improvement. An agricultural labourer, for instance, who in Ireland could expect to earn between 6d and 1s a day could in England get up to 12s a week and as a builder's labourer he could earn between 16s and 18s a week. When employers found that Irish workers were ready to accept less wages than their English fellow-labourers, they were quick to exploit the advantage of having a large pool of cheap labour at their disposal. This was one of the main reasons for the unpopularity of the Irish among the English working-class, who regarded the newcomers as wage-cutters and blacklegs. Textile employers openly used Irish labour to keep down wages or to break strikes. John Guest, a Lancashire cotton manufacturer, was quite frank about this in his evidence to the Committee on the State of the Irish Poor. He said that the constant flood of Irish immigrants kept wages down and drew the teeth of the English trade unions. It is not surprising that there was friction between native and Irish workers, particularly at times of unemployment. On many of the railway construction sites, there were separate encampments for the Irish and English, or Irish and Scots workers, and on several occasions the army had to be called in to quell the fighting.

While the English despised the majority of the Irish for taking low wages, they also had little good to say for those who earned more. They claimed that the Irish were content with poor homes, poor clothing and poor food, and that when they had extra money they just wasted it on useless luxuries, especially drink. But there are other witnesses who tell a different side of the story. Describing the building of the Caledonian Railway near his home in 1846 Thomas Carlyle reported the scenes of disorder among the navvies:

> The Yorkshire and Lancashire men, I hear, are reckoned the worst; and not without glad surprise I find the Irish are the best in point of behaviour. The postman tells me that several of the poor Irish do regularly apply to him for money drafts, and

send their earnings home. The English, who eat twice as much beef, consume the residue in whisky and do not trouble the postman. (Letter of 29 August 1846 to Gavan Duffy.)

The fact is that many of the Irish labouring men had no intention of settling in this country: they were a mobile, seasonal labour force, sending their wages back to their families in Ireland rather than bringing their families over here. This is a pattern which still exists today. These Irish working men were intensely loyal to each other but like most unskilled or casual labourers took little part in trades union activities. Though three of the leaders of the Chartist movement were Irish – John Doherty, Bronterre O'Brien and Feargus O'Connor – in general the immigrants took no part in the English working class movement. Irishmen who had only recently come from conditions of semi-starvation were not much concerned about the political rights of the English worker.

Houses

It has already been pointed out that the Irish immigrants were unprepared for urban living: they were used to the primitive conditions of a peasant cabin and continued to live in the English city as they had done in their Irish village. Housing conditions in the overcrowded cities of Britain were bad enough already, but their arrival undoubtedly helped to make bad slums worse. Much was made of the Irish habit of keeping chickens, goats, pigs, donkeys and dogs with them in their crowded accommodation. The German socialist Engels, writing of Manchester in 1846, reported that the Irishman

builds a pigsty against the house wall as he did at home, and if he is prevented from doing this, he lets the pig sleep in the room with himself. . . . The Irishman loves his pig as the Arab his horse, with the difference that he sells it when it is fat enough to kill. Otherwise he eats and sleeps with it, his children play with it, ride upon it, roll in the dirt with it, as anyone may see a thousand times repeated in all the great towns of England.

Engels' generalisations may be treated with suspicion but it is true that Irish standards of hygiene were low. They used tenement courts as if they were country farmyards: dung was often piled up outside back doors for eventual use as manure. Such conditions were a breeding-ground for disease to which the Irish succumbed easily since they continued to live on the meagre diet of potatoes and buttermilk to which they had been used at home. Moreover, mothers knew little about the proper care of infants.

Conditions in the overcrowded slums of the larger cities were already bad before the bulk of the Irish immigrants arrived in Britain, and the squalor and lack of sanitation were already a matter of public concern. But the fact that the Irish were ready to put up with poor conditions meant that they took over the worst areas in the industrial towns, herding together in colonies or ghettoes with a family to every room. One of the most famous of these areas in London was the 'Rookery' of

St Giles, around what is now the Tottenham Court Road area. Many of the immigrants lived in cellars or in tenements. These wretched lodgings were often airless and lightless since the landlords blocked up the windows to avoid tax. Such conditions, added to the domestic habits described above, were bound to bring about infection and a high mortality rate.

Much was made of the more unusual customs practised by the Irish. For instance, when a death occurred in an Irish family it was usual to hold a 'wake' over the corpse, which remained in the house: family, friends and neighbours gathered to drink in honour of the dead man and to celebrate his memory. This practice was a way of showing respect to the dead and of drawing family and friends together, but it scandalised many English people, who are traditionally more shy of death. They saw the custom as further evidence of Irish barbarism. English officials were also shocked by the close mixing of men, women and children in the crowded lodging-houses. To the immigrants this was a matter of necessity, but there were others who talked darkly of immorality and lack of civilised standards.

Crime

The social conditions in which many of the immigrants lived made it inevitable that many of them gave vent to their frustration in drinking, brawling and violence. Such behaviour was particularly common among the single men who had no family responsibilities. The men from different parts of Ireland such as Connaught (the western counties) and Munster (the southern counties) kept up their traditional rivalries and feuds, and these often erupted into general brawling in which the women and children joined. A Government report of 1835 quotes a Liverpool man as saying: 'The Irish give infinitely more trouble, and are infinitely more riotous and disorderly in the streets, than any other class of persons, or than all others put together; they make a great deal of noise, they are in fact more accustomed to a country than a town life.' (*Report on the State of the Irish Poor in England*, p. 20.) The image of the 'flailing Paddy' hitting out with his shillelagh still persists today.

One thing the Irish had learned back home was a disrespect for the police. Sir Robert Peel's establishment of a police force in Ireland in 1814 had been seen by the Irish as an attempt to tighten English authority in their country. We have seen that Peel's efforts to introduce a police system in England also met with opposition and nowhere was this stronger than amongst the immigrant Irish, many of whom had experienced the operation of the system on their home ground.

Not many of the Irish were professional criminals, but in the poorer areas, as might be expected, there was a high incidence of petty crime, pilfering and pickpocketing, particularly among the young. Exact figures are not available, but many observers comment on the high percentage of children of Irish origin among young prisoners. According to one estimate, in 1868 one fifth of the gaol population of England and Wales were Irish.

Religion

One of the main reasons for English prejudice against the Irish immigrants was that the Irish were Roman Catholics. Anti-Catholic feeling was still strong in nineteenth century England. In 1778 the first moves to restore civil rights to Catholics had led to violent mob disturbances (the 'Gordon riots'), fed by popular rumours of a Catholic plot to overthrow Protestantism and restore the Pope. The Church of Rome was still denounced as the Scarlet Woman, and Catholics regarded as an alien and sinister minority whose patriotism was suspect because they owed allegiance to the Pope of Rome. In 1853 *The Times* wrote in an editorial, 'We very much doubt whether in England, or indeed in any free Protestant country, a true Papist can be a good subject.' The Catholic Emancipation Bill in 1829 was only passed in the teeth of strong popular opposition, and there was a further outbreak of anti-Catholic feeling in 1851, sparked off by the restoration of the Roman Catholic hierarchy in England and Wales: effigies of the Pope and the Catholic Archbishop of Westminster were publicly burnt in the streets.

Until the nineteenth century Catholics in England had been a small minority, shunning the limelight and eager to prove their loyalty to the Crown. Many of them belonged to old landowning families who had kept the 'old faith' alive in the chapels of their great houses. These English Catholics regarded their Irish co-religionists with the embarrassment a respectable citizen feels on the arrival of a disreputable and noisy relative who has to be apologised for and explained away to friends and neighbours. Irish Catholicism was no private, genteel affair: it was essentially a people's religion, a religion of the poor. Deprived of political leadership during long years of oppression, the Irish people had turned for inspiration to the Church: the spirit of the Irish nation found its expression in and through Irish Catholicism.

In the early part of the nineteenth century the spiritual welfare of Irish immigrants was sadly neglected, but gradually chapels were built in the centres of Irish settlement, with priests to serve them. While many of the immigrants no longer practised their religion formally, the sense of belonging to the Church community gave them status and security. The priest could exercise more influence in these areas than ever the law or the police could. Thus the Irish Catholic community developed its own social life, often isolated from the larger community around it. This further aroused the hostility of the native English and when anti-Irish disturbances broke out they were often directed at the Roman Catholic church or chapel as being the symbol of the Irish community. In 1848 for instance the murder by an Irish navvy of a young Welshman in Cardiff led to a mob attack on the Catholic church and priest's house there, during which the police and militia took no action to protect the property of the Irish or to arrest the rioters.

Attitudes towards the Immigrants
Many Irishmen were driven to England by sheer force of economic necessity, but they did not easily integrate in the country in which they had to earn their living. The reluctance of the Irish to commit themselves to the political and social system of Britain meant that they were regarded as dangerous aliens – 'a population living in the midst of us, but estranged from our religion, our laws, our manners and our government', as one contemporary put it (J. Garwood, *The Million Peopled City*, p. 269). These fears of Irish subversion increased later in the century when revolutionary societies such as the Fenians and the Irish Republican Brotherhood extended

YOUNG IRELAND IN BUSINESS FOR HIMSELF.

Young Ireland in business for himself.
A *Punch* cartoon of 1846, reflecting the fears aroused by the growth of Irish nationalism and the 'Young Ireland' movement. Nineteenth century cartoons usually portray the Irishman either as a comic peasant ('Paddy') or as an ape-like animal. This picture suggests something between the two — a mischievous chimpanzee.

their activities into England: *Punch* cartoons of the 1860s depict these agitators as brutal ape-men, belonging to a race of sub-human monsters. In fact the fears were groundless because the majority of Irish in England had little sympathy with revolutionary or republican aims.

133

Attitudes towards the Immigrants

Hostility towards the immigrants was an emotion which united the middle classes and working classes of England. The main reason for the working man's distrust was simple: the Irish were taking the bread out of his mouth. Middle class critics adopted a more moral tone. To them, the immigrants seemed to be a threat to the whole British way of life. The Irish were uncivilised and unhealthy; they lived in dirt, in foul slums; they were drunkards; they caused riots and disorders; they would drag down lower orders of society to their own level. These opinions, voiced in newspapers and official reports, were often taken over, in an exaggerated form, by less-educated people: 'We are accustomed to associate notions of filth, squalor and beggarly destitution with everything *Irish* from the large number of lazy, idle and wretched natives of the Sister Island who are continually crossing our paths.' (*The Cardiff Advertiser and Merthyr Guardian*, March 1850.) Later in the century, Karl Marx compared the attitude of the English worker to the Irish immigrants with that of the 'poor whites' to the 'niggers' in the southern states of the USA.

It was not the immigrant who brought slums, dirt and disease, starvation wages, disorder and poverty to Britain. All these problems were there already. What the Irish did was to make these problems worse and more obvious. The Irish community was a kind of distorting mirror in which the Englishman could see the unacceptable face of his own society twisted and magnified. It is no wonder that the immigrants were the victims of violent and irrational prejudice. A modern writer has put the idea well:

> It is clear from the experience of the nineteenth century that many of the weaknesses which the immigrants' situation exposed were weaknesses in the fabric, structure and ideology of the host society. The situation is the same today when the pressure of change represented by the immigrants in Britain of whatever race, religion or nationality, exposes and threatens the weaknesses, prejudice, fears and frustrations of the British people. (J. A. Jackson, *The Irish in Britain*, p. 70.)

ORIGINAL SOURCES

Report of the Select Committee on Railway Labourers. Parliamentary Papers Vol. XXII, 1846.
Report on the State of the Irish Poor in Great Britain. Parliamentary Papers XXXIV, 1836.

FURTHER READING

Coleman, Terry. *The Railway Navvies.* Hutchinson, London, 1965.
Curtis, L. P. *Anglo-Saxons and Celts: A Study of the Anti-Irish Prejudice in Victorian England.* New York University Press, New York, 1968.
Hickey, John. *Urban Catholics.* Chapman, London, 1965. A useful study of the history of the Irish Catholic community in Cardiff.
Jackson, J. A. *The Irish in Britain.* Routledge, London, 1963. An excellent and comprehensive survey.

Norman, E. R. *Anti-Catholicism in Victorian England*. Allen & Unwin, London, 1968.
Woodham-Smith, Cecil. *The Great Hunger*. Hamish Hamilton, London, 1962.

LITERARY SOURCES

Dickens, Charles. *Oliver Twist*. Penguin, Harmondsworth, 1970. (Chapter 8: the St Giles Rookery.)
Gaskell, Elizabeth. *North and South*. Penguin, Harmondsworth, 1970. (Chapters 18 and 22: use of the Irish as strike-breakers.)
Morrison, Arthur. *A Child of the Jago*. Panther, London, 1971. (Chapter 5: a fight in a London rookery.)

Conclusion

WE HAVE SEEN THAT WITH THE INDUSTRIAL REVOLUTION THERE CAME A PROBLEM OF population. The number of people living in Great Britain increased dramatically in little more than two generations. Moreover, they flooded into the towns, which grew at a rate out of all proportion to that of the countryside. In the late eighteenth century the British were, for the most part, country dwellers: by 1850 half of them lived in towns. This was a great event in the history of the world, for the first large-scale, urban society had been born. But because it was quite new the authorities, central and local, did not know how to cope. While they fumbled for solutions the problems grew, and there developed all the evils that we have studied chapter by chapter in this book.

Many of these problems are still with us and some of our worst difficulties are a direct inheritance from the Industrial Revolution. However, there is another side to the picture. There were few evils that appeared in the early nineteenth century that did not have the opposition of determined men. They ranged from the peculiar fanatics of the temperance movement, through the ordinary clergy and doctors to men like James Philip Kay, Edwin Chadwick and Lord Ashley. In each chapter we have been able to see not only a bad social problem, but also the beginnings, at least, of some attempts to solve it.

Biographical notes

ALTHORP, LORD See Spencer, John Charles.

ASHLEY, Lord See Cooper, Anthony Ashley.

BELL, ANDREW 1753–1832

Andrew Bell was an unattractive character being vain, overbearing, and above all, miserly. He was good at finding himself jobs which brought high salaries and practically no work, and this left him ample opportunity to create a reputation for himself as a great educational reformer.

He was the son of a barber, but laid the foundations of his own career by becoming a clergyman in the Church of England. In 1787 he went to India and occupied the posts of eight army chaplains! Though he drew eight salaries, he did very little work and found plenty of time to devote to his pet project, the Madras Male Orphan Asylum. Here he found problems for he had a large number of difficult half-caste children and only a handful of ill-paid teachers. It was this which led him to develop the monitorial system, which, because of his enthusiasm and organising ability, was a success.

In 1796 he returned to England with £25 000 and the conviction that he had invented a wonderful new system of education.

In 1797 he published his ideas in a book called *An Experiment in Education made at the Male Asylum of Madras* and in the following year he introduced his system in a Charity School, St Botolph's, Aldgate.

In 1801 he became Rector of Swanage, again with a good stipend, but, since he neglected his parish, plenty of spare time.

In 1803 he first came into contact with the Quaker, Joseph Lancaster, who was also developing the monitorial system. After a short period of enthusiastic co-operation the two quarrelled, partly over details of the way they thought schools should be organised, but mainly over religion.

Bell's period of success began in 1811 with the formation of the National Society of which he was the Superintendent. This meant that the Church of England had adopted his system and he had the satisfaction of seeing it spread far and wide.

In the end the monitorial schools were shown to be inadequate, but they were the beginning of a national system of education. Bell, and his rival Lancaster, were important pioneers.

Biographical notes

CHADWICK, EDWIN, 1800–1880

Chadwick was important for his work connected with the care of the poor and public health. An account of his public life is given in Chapters Two and Six.

He was forced into premature retirement at the age of fifty-four and then lived to be eighty. He produced a considerable volume of writing in those years but to little avail. His ability was considerable: he was sincere, dedicated and hard working, but his personality was such that his excellent ideas were rejected by others. He was above all else a tedious bore and no one was willing to listen to him.

COOPER, ANTHONY ASHLEY, SEVENTH EARL OF SHAFTESBURY 1801–1885

The Earl of Shaftesbury was one of the greatest philanthropists of the nineteenth century, and devoted his life to bettering the condition of the working classes. He was, none the less, an odd character and not at all easy in his relations with others. His parents neglected him as a child and it may well have been that his philanthropic work was a quest for the recognition and affection that he had missed in early life.

He was incapable of handling money and when he inherited his father's estates in Dorset he was already £100 000 in debt. He did not find the estate at all in good order and consequently the labourers there lived in conditions as squalid as any that Shaftesbury discovered and tried to put right in the industrial towns. His enemies were not slow to point this out. Shaftesbury was well aware of the problem, and, not surprisingly, sensitive about it, but he lacked the business acumen to put it right.

In some ways he was reactionary. Being a Tory landlord, he opposed Parliamentary reform, supported the Corn Laws and disliked trade unions. Yet he had an impressive record of public service. The following were his main activities:

The reform of the lunacy laws. His Act of 1845 ensured that lunatics had to be properly certified and then cared for in well-conducted asylums.

The Ten Hours Movement – see Chapter Five.

Reform of the mines – see Chapter Five.

Public Health – see Chapter Two.

Protection of women and children in agriculture. He was largely responsible for an Act of 1873 which regulated gang labour.

Protection of child chimney sweeps. This was achieved by two Acts of Parliament, one in 1864 and one in 1875.

Care of destitute children. He started Ragged Schools, organised schemes for training neglected children, and helping them to emigrate. He also started the Shaftesbury homes.

FIELDEN, JOHN 1784–1849

The Fieldens were one of those families who, like the Peels, began as yeomen farmers producing textiles as a side-line and later became extremely wealthy cotton manufacturers.

John Fielden began his career as a partner with his father, who was both farmer and cotton spinner. In 1811 he joined with his brothers to set up the Waterside Mills at Todmorden. Soon the firm of Fielden Brothers was one of the largest in the country. The new factories made a fortune for the Fieldens but John was the bitter enemy of factory owners and the author of a book called *The Curse of the Factory System*. Yet he was not unique, as we can see from the lives of Robert Peel Senior and Robert Owen.

In 1832 the Reform Act made Oldham one of the new Parliamentary Boroughs and in the following year Fielden and his friend William Cobbett were elected as its Members of Parliament. In Parliament Fielden became one of the leaders of the Ten Hours Movement and was the man largely responsible for the Act of 1847.

FRY, ELIZABETH (Née Gurney) 1780–1845

The Gurney family was from Norfolk and they were wealthy woollen manufacturers and bankers. Although they were Quakers, Elizabeth led rather a gay youth but she was converted to a more serious outlook by the preaching of an American called Savery.

She started by caring for the poor on the family estates and then went on to her work for the reform of the prisons (see Chapter Nine).

In 1800 she married another Quaker, Joseph Fry. For a time the family was prosperous and this left Elizabeth free for her good works. However, Joseph Fry went bankrupt in 1828 and this was a serious setback for his wife. Yet she still continued to do all she could, helping not only prisoners but others in need, particularly the homeless poor.

HUNT, HENRY 1773–1835

Hunt was a great mob orator, but a failure at almost everything else. He was a violent and objectionable man.

He was the son of a Wiltshire farmer and tried to make a living in the same way, but without success. He carried on a series of law suits with his neighbours and spent some time in prison for assaulting a game-keeper.

He took to politics as a radical, in favour of such things as universal manhood suffrage and vote by ballot. His violent temperament helped him become an excellent speaker, particularly before large crowds in the open air. The meeting at St Peter's Fields in 1819 was typical of such gatherings. For his part in this, Hunt served two years imprisonment.

After many attempts to get into Parliament he became M.P. for Preston in 1831. In 1833 he lost his seat and spent the few remaining years of his life manufacturing boot blacking.

HOWARD, JOHN 1726–1790

Howard's father was an upholsterer, and also owned a small estate at Cardington in Bedfordshire.

Howard's work was done under the strain of an unhappy private life and, not surprisingly, he was a strange, shy, withdrawn man, who had difficulty in making friends. But he had tremendous determination and when in his late forties he saw the need for prison reform nothing could turn him from it. He claimed that he travelled 50 000 miles in Europe, visiting all the gaols, hospitals and quarantine stations he could.

Biographical notes

In 1774 he gave evidence to the House of Commons and in 1777 wrote his *State of the Prisons* which was to have great influence.

He died in Russia, from a disease he caught while visiting a hospital in an army camp.

KAY-SHUTTLEWORTH, SIR JAMES 1804–1877

His family name was Kay and he changed his name when he married Janet Shuttleworth in 1842.

Kay-Shuttleworth studied medicine at Edinburgh and then practised in Manchester where he devoted himself to the welfare of the working classes. He became Medical Officer to the Ancoats and Ardwick Dispensary, and Secretary to the Manchester Board of Health. In 1832 he helped fight the cholera epidemic, and what this taught him about the poor led him to write his book, *Moral and Physical Condition of the Working Classes employed in the Cotton Manufacture in Manchester*.

In 1835 he became an Assistant Poor Law Commissioner and this stimulated his interest in education, since he had to face the problem of training pauper children. In 1839 he became Secretary of the newly formed Committee of Council for Education. Here his most important work was with the training of teachers (see Chapter Ten).

His health broke down under pressure of work and in 1849 he retired from the Committee of Council for Education and returned to Lancashire. He still went on helping the poor, as for example when he did relief work during the cotton famine.

LANCASTER, JOSEPH 1778–1838

Joseph Lancaster was the son of a shopkeeper; he was a Quaker, and took his religion seriously from an early age.

In 1801 he opened a school in Borough Road, London. He collected fees from those who wanted to pay, but any boy could attend for nothing. He could not afford adult teachers, so he developed a system of teaching with the aid of monitors. He did this a short time after Andrew Bell but made his own discovery quite independently. He and Bell co-operated for a while, but then disagreed over religion.

In 1803 Lancaster published his ideas in his book *Improvements in Education*. Soon he was attracting a lot of attention, and George III himself met Lancaster and agreed to give a subscription to his school.

Unlike his rival Bell, Lancaster could not manage money and by 1808 he was in trouble. Two of his fellow Quakers put things right and also set up the Royal Lancasterian Society to administer his affairs. Lancaster could not work under anyone else so he left the society and, after a spell in prison for debt, he migrated to America. Here he started several schools and as each one failed he moved somewhere else. He died in New York as the result of a street accident in 1838.

Lancaster once boasted that with properly trained monitors he could teach 10 000 children to read within three months, but the monitorial system was soon proved to be inadequate. However, it was Lancaster and Bell who first tackled the problem of full-time education for all children. Others learnt from their experience and from this our national system of education developed.

OASTLER, RICHARD 1789–1861

Richard Oastler was the son of the steward of the Fixby estates in Yorkshire which belonged to a family called Thornhill. When his father died in 1820 Richard took over the job.

Oastler was a member of the Church of England, and in politics he was a Tory and a supporter of the Corn Laws. But like so many supporters of the agricultural interest he fought vigorously for the reform of the factories.

For some time he was interested in freeing the slaves in the English colonies, but in 1830 a friend told him about child labour in the Yorkshire woollen mills. Oastler decided that Yorkshire children were treated worse than West Indian slaves and this led to his famous article in the *Leeds Mercury*. From then on he led the Ten Hours Movement in Yorkshire, working in close contact with men like Sadler who were leading it in Parliament.

His employer approved of his work for factory reform, but when he opposed the application of the new Poor Law, Thornhill dismissed him. This was a double misfortune for Oastler owed his former employer £2000. He spent three years as a debtor in the Fleet Prison until his friends raised a subscription to pay the money he owed.

OWEN, ROBERT 1771–1858

Owen was the son of a Welsh sadler. He started his working life as a shop assistant, and saved enough money to open a very small factory. He then gave this up in order to be manager of a much larger works. His big chance came when, with a group of other businessmen, he bought the New Lanark Mills. Owen first of all made these mills highly efficient, and then used the profits to provide what were, for those days, ideal conditions for the workers.

The mills were ventilated and made safe; the workers had good houses that they were encouraged to keep clean; the factory settlement had a store, and its streets were well-paved and scavenged. There was also an unofficial police force. Offenders were fined by deductions from their wages and the money went to pay for medical treatment for the sick. But probably the most important development was in education. At New Lanark they had the first of the factory schools, and every child under ten had to attend full-time, being forbidden to work in the mill. Adults could go to school too, after their day's work was over.

As a factory manager and reformer, Owen was successful, but his grandiose schemes for the regeneration of society as a whole came to nothing. He set out his ideas in his book *A New View of Society* and then tried them out, first of all in the trade union movement and then in the co-operative movement. This is described in Chapter Eight.

PEEL, SIR ROBERT 1788–1850

There were three Robert Peels — grandfather, father and son. The eldest was a yeoman farmer, manufacturing textiles as a side line. He laid the foundations of the family's fortunes by discovering a new way of printing calico and they became prosperous cotton manufacturers.

Biographical notes

The second Robert Peel was a Member of Parliament and was responsible for the first Act for the protection of factory children (see Chapter Five).

It was the third Robert Peel who became really famous. He entered Parliament in 1809, and by 1812 he held an important office, First Secretary for Ireland. Here he gained important experience in the organisation of a police force when he formed the Royal Irish Constabulary.

In 1833 he was Home Secretary in Lord Liverpool's Government and was responsible for reforms in criminal law, which abolished the death penalty for a great many offences. He also caused Parliament to pass the Gaol Act of 1823 (see Chapter Nine). Later, as a member of Wellington's Government, he was responsible for the Metropolitan Police Act of 1829 (see Chapter Nine).

Also in 1829 Peel had a great deal to do with the Act for Catholic Emancipation, which gave Catholics the same civic rights as Protestants.

From 1841 to 1846 he was Prime Minister and his chief work during this time was to complete, virtually, the change in the commercial policy of this country to one of free trade. He revived income tax – at sevenpence in the pound – so that the government would have an alternative revenue, and then went on to abolish most of the tariffs on imported goods.

For some time there was one item that he dared not touch and this was corn. Peel was a Tory, and his party represented the landed interest. Landowners wanted import duties on foreign corn to keep up the price of wheat grown in this country, and Peel had come to power pledged to support this policy. He changed his own views, but knew he could not persuade his party to change theirs. However, the Irish potato famine made it essential to have an abundant supply of cheap corn and in 1846 Peel secured the repeal of the Corn Laws. His enemies in his own party then combined with the Whigs to drive him from power and he never again held office.

RAIKES, ROBERT 1735–1811
Raikes was the son of a Gloucester printer and he followed the same occupation.

He was concerned for the welfare of the people of his town, including the inmates of the gaol. It was he who entertained John Howard when he visited Gloucester to see the prison.

Raikes's most important work was with Sunday Schools. It was certainly not a new idea to teach children on Sundays and indeed Raikes had the help of a curate, Thomas Stock, who had already organised a Sunday School in Berkshire. Raikes and Stock opened a school in Gloucester in 1780, and as Raikes was a printer it was easy for him to spread the news of his scheme. By now people recognised that it was important to educate everyone and Sunday Schools sprang up all over the country.

SENIOR, NASSAU WILLIAM 1790–1864
Nassau Senior was one of the leading figures in a group of people calling themselves Political Economists.

The son of a clergyman at Durnford in Wiltshire, Senior went to Eton and then to Oxford. In 1812 he joined Lincoln's Inn intending to become a barrister, which was a strange career to choose as he had a delicate throat and a feeble voice.

Not surprisingly, nothing came of his legal career and he turned to political economy. He became well known for his work and in 1853 was made a member of the Commission that reported on the Poor Laws.

Later he served on other Commissions, for example, the Factory Commission of 1837, but in public life he did not get any further. He was offered several important positions but declined them all, preferring to devote his time to his writing and studying.

SHAFTESBURY — SEVENTH EARL OF See Cooper, Anthony Ashley.

SPENCER, JOHN CHARLES (Lord Althorp) 1782–1845

Lord Althorp was a man who came close to having 'greatness thrust upon him'. He did only moderately well at school and was quiet, reserved and diffident throughout his life. But he also had real ability, integrity and high qualities of character.

Although born into a Tory family, Althorp became a Whig. He became M.P. for Okehampton in 1804, but later stood for Northamptonshire, which he represented for twenty-eight years.

In 1830 he became leader of the Whigs, which meant that he should have been Prime Minister as soon as they won a general election. However, when this happened later the same year, he refused the position and chose instead to serve under Grey, becoming Chancellor of the Exchequer and Leader of the House of Commons.

Althorp's most important political contribution was the support he gave to the Reform Bill of 1832, but like many serious-minded men of his time he was aware of the social problems which followed the Napoleonic Wars. This made him a suitable man to guide the Factories Regulation Act through Parliament (see Chapter Five).

Index

Index

Index

Index